I0623452

Legend *of* Bread

Ana Doina

Legacy Book Press LLC
Camanche, Iowa

For my children and grandchildren

Table of Contents

Accent

The whispers of my childhood woods
and the hills redundantly green
cast a blade-sharp curse on my tongue—
*the rich earth's crust, the salt-thick sea,
the verdant domes, the verdant domes
you'll never inherit!* As if space
becomes litany and landscape
layers its coherence
on sounds.

After Yalta

Although
the streets were left unlit, and centuries-old
buildings, forsaken, darkened with grime;

although
in squalid government-funded houses
a chorus of housewives lamented
the lack of cold cuts and the scarcity
of money, while peasants sold
wilted dill in gloomy open markets;

although
banished words like *sir* and *madam*
were replaced by *comrade*, curfew imposed,
weddings outlawed after midnight;

although
rum was plentiful, sugar and soap rationed,
the Bible prohibited, legendary churches
demolished, monuments to Lenin and Stalin
built in their stead, the menacing Russkies,
armed to the gills with rifles and tanks,
always and forever at the border;

although
the world, divided, abandoned one of its halves
behind the Iron Curtain to iron fists, *kirza* boots,
broken treaties, then forgot about it, and grew
prosperous on a well-executed Marshall Plan;

here,
in the Eastern Bloc countries,
where the hastily manufactured
Communist Revolution
turned into a grotesque mix of terror
and gallows humor,

music
was still played, jokes copious, and people
fell in love, had children, got divorced,
just as in any other part of the world.

Iron Curtain

At Buchenwald, the clock stopped
at 3:15. Was it early morning
or mid afternoon? Who remembers?

What became clear to all
this time was that *Jedem
das Seine,* the forged-

iron slogan above the death
camp's gates, told—*to each
its own* bigger, better bombs,

while an opaque curtain descended
its terror and gloom over ancient towns,
time froze in an unending war

dividing the world into two enemy words:
them and *us*, as if there wasn't ever
going to be a friendly neighbor again.

Home, a chant

A shadow captured in family pictures;
a soothing chant for tribal belonging;
measured spaces of peace; a longing
for holiday's aroma, for breakfast milk;
home
a legend of bread bought at the corner store
when, too young to know the value of money,
I thought the silver change was so much more;
footnote ingrained by life on accents, in tones; dolls,
cradles, symbols of love; collection of weddings;
grapes swollen into wine to flower on Mother's
outgrown wedding dress, on Father's faithlessness
hemmed with mistresses sleeping in his dreams;
home
with children spread like ivy on the family tree;
furniture moved with divorces in a step-by-step
dance toward acquired brothers and cousins;
aunts reciting gospels of childhood wrongs;
the wrinkles Mother's hands turned into
my growing; a womb that defies
the peeling of time;
home
ceremonial lies said
to plaster good mornings on top
of good nights; family secrets mentioned
only in gestures cast over growth, grievances,
treasures; a hug before sleep, and a gaze
walking me over crossroads; conversations
left unfolded to finish when older;

home
a perpetual door
I could open without any resistance,
even if behind it the air was heavy
with contradictions and crystal vases
shattered after a fight; bruised knees,
and the fences I stubbornly broke through
to steal sweet cherries, sensual
like the month of July;
the place I come back to, expecting
grandparents' features repeated on youngsters,
and a chocolate cake baked to honor my return
to the grief of departures;
the trees I've planted and the ones
I've used to fence rituals holding together
the silver coins returned as change.
Home.

Romanian village, 1946

for Dr. John Gilgun

One day, Uncle sent us to fetch
a bucket of argyle, the wet ash-colored clay
he could use to make the much-needed pots
for the kitchen, a small doll just for me,
and a flute for my brother.

He said to go past the last rows of peach trees
in the orchard, near the small cemetery,
where thick blades of grass change to dense moss
and the forest begins its quiet and tall growth
from earth's dark velvet.

Right there we found the stranger—
the round shape of his helmet shone in the sun
like the back of a tortoise. The buzz of insects
and the sickening smell dizzied and entrapped us.
Muckworms squirmed through his flesh.

Nothing of him was left whole
but his helmet and boots. "Not a sight for a girl!"
Brother said. "God knows how many days
he's been dead." We went back empty-handed
and scared. But soon the whole village
came to see the dead man. Children and grandmas
rushed first, then women and men left their fields
to flock to the spot where a body lay
covered in clay, God only knew for how long.

The men said he must have been a soldier,
given his helmet and his boots, no doubt
a German, left there during retreat.

My aunt covered him with a peacock shrug
she had woven a few years back, during the war,
and someone was sent for the priest. But the priest
didn't know what to do. "If he is a German,"
the good Father said, numbering prayers
on the argyle beads of a rosary,
"he's not of our rite."

There was no way to know who he was,
where he came from, who he fought for.
We knew he was young by his bones
and his teeth. Maybe a peasant, or a shepherd,
like us. No rankings, no insignia, nothing
distinctive was found in the mud
near the corpse. So we dug a grave at the edge
of the forest, in the small cemetery,
in the last row. We gave him a proper burial,
without his name and the birth-right ritual
of mourning.

The priest led a mixed ceremony
with prayer words from all the Christian rites,
making the sign of the cross from right to left for us,
and left to right as he thought the dead man
would have done, and we prayed
for the souls of all mothers and fathers and sons
lost on other foreign lands.

We laid the German,
this unknown stranger, this enemy, near our own
dead soldiers.

Next day, Brother and I had to go past
the last row of peach trees in the orchard
to fetch some potter's clay. Uncle came with us
and, touching the argillaceous earth
with his agile fingers, he said—"This must be
the best clay in the world."

And I knew he would make a vase of this clay,
oval-shaped like a nursing breast, like a tear,
like a continuous enclosing horizon.

Top-Secret Report

Babitchka, your cooking habits
became the talk of the town,
Bucharest winter of '59.

Even the Secret Police
spied on you and Frau Rappaport,
trafficking plates of food and dirty dishes
between Hope Street and Lenin Lane.

One day, two well-dressed fellows
brought trembling Frau Rappaport
to your door to have a little talk
with you two. The four of you sat
around your round ebony table
eating homemade peach pie, sipping
sour-cherry brandy, as you explained
that, since the Mayor divided your house
between seven families, still displaced
this many years after the war, you lost
your large kitchen to a Gypsy clan
who slept and cooked there.

In the bedroom closet-turned-kitchen
you only cook dairy and vegetables now,
while in her house, Frau Rappaport
takes care of the meat.

Another day, the same fellows
took you to Frau Rappaport's
to explain why the dirty dishes
go from house to house, and you said,

as if it should have been obvious—
"Well, think about it, young man.
How can I wash meat dishes
in my dairy sink?"

The fellows wrote to their superior
secret policeman: *We found no*
subversive activity going on
between Hope Street and Lenin Lane.
The Citizens, Katz (woman, 65 years old)
and Rappaport (woman, 54 years old)
are trying to keep kosher,
nothing more.

Meteor shower

Out one summer evening
well past a five-year-old's bedtime,
my stepmother told me to look at the sky,
watch the meteor shower above our heads.
"If you see a falling star," she said,
"make a wish!" I wished for her death.

And immediately felt frightened
and damned. I knew right from wrong,
I knew how evil it was to wish
for someone else's death, I could feel
the awful weight of my sin crushing me,
turning me into an odious creature, and still,
with each falling star, I kept on wishing.

Tall, dark-haired, imposing
she revisits my thoughts
when I least expect it, even now,
though she has not been part
of my life for so many decades.

She's there, in the folds of my mind.
Her insidious voice still colors my days.
My flogged skin still burns along the faint scars
left by the whip she used to lash me
for losing my mittens, or refusing my spinach.

Yet I am the one still overwhelmed by shame
and the guilt of my own long-ago sinful hatred
every time I see a falling star.

Father figure

The larger chunk of meat,
the softer part of bread, given
to *him*, after a back-breaking
day at the office.

I had to keep quiet,
not disturb *his* papers,
his slippers,
not play with *his* tools,
as if *he* had exalted
everything *he* owned
to sainthood.

O, how many times
did I grab the bread
before he could have it,
kicked his slippers
under the bed, watched him
get on his knees,
searching
for what should have been
orderly there.

I liked how he looked
needy and uncomfortable,
slumped over the bed,
blindly feeling the floor
for a familiar shape.

He'd narrow his eyes
as if looking through a needle
and ask, "Did you do this on purpose?"

I'd straighten my starched skirt,
cover my knees, look respectable,
like a lady, and change the subject,
as if his authority were something
I'd never question.

Memorabilia

for Alin and Filip

Awaken
with the open door
sensories of Buni's[1] home
bread and flowers,
orange peels, apples
set on windowsills
hibernating till next pie.
Time
on pendulum's
measured rhythm,
stories told on sepia colors,
and the sniff of sweet tobacco
enveloped with stamp collections.
Objects borrowed on the meanings
and the tides now just recalled,
lavendered linens kept vacations
for successive generations.
Pillows,
pillows, were ancestors
ever-present and imposing
from the pictures
took a nap.

[1]Affectionate name for *grandmother* in Romanian

Chronic lateness

"Leave the house
a quarter hour earlier,"
she'd say, exasperated
by my showing up to class
ten minutes late, again and again.
She looked at me over her glasses,
and under her gaze I felt awkward
and squirmed while the kids in the class
snickered sanctimoniously.

The teacher sent me to my seat
before I could ever explain that *that*
was actually the problem,
that quarter hour allowed me to think
there was so much I could cram into it
before the school day started.

"Leave at a quarter to eight
and you'll make it on time!"
the teacher said. "There are only
three short blocks between your house
and the school!" True, but what she didn't
count on were shoelaces suddenly undone,
dropped books, the oh-so-good-looking
boy next door asking *me*
about the latest school gossip.

What she didn't count on
were the cute kittens
sunning on a windowsill,
or the flowers I had to stop for

and take in a good sniff of,
or the lost dog in need of rescue,
while all my schoolmates
were already greeting
the teacher.

The boy next door

What was his name? One year my junior,
he had our whole life planned ahead for us.

I thought he was too young for me, tradition
insisted the husband had to be older
than the wife, but he was cute
and I felt safe around him.

He said we'd marry on some future May Day
and that he'd love me forever. He'd be a pilot,
like his dad, travel the world, while I, at home,
would take care of our brilliant, happy children.

We held hands out in the park
when far from spying neighbors. I was eight,
my mother had just remarried a frightful
boor of a man, my father was divorcing
his sadistic second wife.

Once, sitting on the lower step
of the gently rising staircase
inside a cool dark hallway, I let him
kiss me, furtively, on my cheek.

His plans sounded like the end of a fairytale,
the realm of quiet that comes after troubles
and bloodcurdling quests.

A few months later, his mother left his father
and moved away, taking the boy with her
someplace I've never known where
and I never heard from him again.

How does forever feel, I wondered one morning
while chasing a whirlwind of autumn leaves
out in the park, wishing to be seized by the swirl
of gold and copper foliage and be lifted
to the windy sky, out, out and away from this
uncertain world.

Stealing cherries in the month of July

The lush moss patch under the cherry tree
was the only soft spot in the garden.
Any other place and you would have gotten
a scraped knee, a twisted ankle, landing
on rocks bordering flower beds, evergreens,
herb patches.

Somehow, even after all the summers
and the generations of kids stealing
his cherries the very day they turned sweet,
year after year, the old, unfriendly gardener
had not figured it out!

We'd hang from branches, grab red ripe orbs,
climb limb by limb with stained faces, stained
fingers, one ear cocked to hear his heavy steps,
eyes watching to see him come, with a broomstick
in his hand, dragging his war-injured leg.
With a mouthful of curses, he slowly made his way
to the tree to try and save his fruits from our
thieving hands, from our insatiable cravings.

We thought ourselves clever, one by one landing
on the soft moss, scurrying away, happy to escape
unpunished, cherry juice still dripping
from our laughing mouths; yet we never realized
that the angry gardener did not go after the one kid
caught in the branches, the slow one left behind,
the frightened child.

Daedalus

Telling the story of Daedalus, the father—
master of labyrinths, of double-edged axes
and magical statues—you carried me through
dark streets covered in crushed linden flowers.

It was harvest time, but in our
prosaic era no soothsayers were left to inhale
the hypnotic scent and transcend into a future
only their eyes could understand. The sacred
flowers rotted on the asphalt, a nuisance.

Heady with the fragrant night, curled up
on your shoulder, my feet wrapped
in the sandals you made for me resting
on your belt buckle, I listened to the sweet
persuasion in your voice: "Daedalus,
held captive on a white Cretan hill, built
wings made of feathers and wax for him
and his child, and escaped."

We looked like any other family—a father,
his young child of five or six, thrilled to be
awake late, returning from a family feast.
We crossed the street at the Icarus Monument.

"Daedalus's child," you continued,
"wished to reach higher than his wings
allowed." The cadence of your words turned
the ill-fated flight into a sacrifice to high
aspirations—praiseworthy ideal.

        You were the father bringing marvels
into the world, and I strived to embody
all the enchanting legends you told.

        But as I grew, the myth changed
in your telling. "Icarus was ungrateful,
did not listen to Daedalus's advice, did not keep
the wise middle ground of a cautious flight.
The fall was Faith's well-deserved punishment
for reaching too far."

        Making my own way out of the labyrinth,
with each chaotic vertigo of a perilous journey
on weak wings, I am leaving behind your world,
savagely crushing linden flowers under the sandals
you made for me, while you rage against cruel gods
punishing a wretched father, as if a lost flight
roars within you its cursed soaring.

Ich bin ein Berliner

My birthday present—the black-and-white
images on the tubular TV Mom brought
into the living room: soldiers lined up,
a newly spun barbed wire dividing streets,
and the still-smoldering war in Berlin.

At first one could jump over the fence;
then a wall was built, but people still jumped
from windows of west-facing buildings
over to what became known as freedom
but was only the other side of the street.

One day soldiers in battle order and the world
stood watch over Peter Fechter, gunned down
on the wall for having tried to jump it.
To tell you the truth, it wasn't easy to feel sorry
for them, the Germans; served them right,
their turn to suffer, divided and mouse-trapped.

Nuclear shadows loomed, Khrushchev
took to pounding the heel of his shoe
at the United Nations General Assembly.
Newspapers counted the many times
Russia could blow up the world,
announcing America could do it
twofold. We became a *brave new world*.

From China to Jerusalem, to Berlin
fenced in by incompatible principles,
we faced wailing walls—cold
like Peter Fechter's slow death.

And now the Wall is coming down
as if it were made of LEGOs.
I watch it on TV. People dance on the Wall,
hammer it down, tear off pieces of plaster,
soldiers toss their guns and join in the dance.
Free. Only I still mourn Peter Fechter.

Gagarin's radishes

From that day on,
we called them Gagarin's radishes.
Ms. Elsy, our neighbor, had a garden
full of them, and to enlist some quick
young hands she promised
sandwiches for helping
with the harvest. Six of us,
eight- and nine-year-olds
playing hopscotch on the street,
accepted, knowing how generous
Ms. Elsy was with water and fruit
on summer days, when, sweaty
or hungry, we stopped by her gate
and called on her daughters
to come out to play.

White, pink, and red, globular roots
came out of the crumbling clumps
of May's earth with ease,
and we could smell the wholesome
taste and the crisp texture even before
the sandwiches were made of steaming
homemade bread layered with butter
and thin round slices of new radishes
sprinkled with thick salt.

Ms. Elsy's new black-and-white TV
was on, and while we sat down to eat,
we watched a Soviet documentary
about conquering Space.

The frightening darkness
of a hostile universe,
the raids of untamed comets,
the fire-spitting rockets sent to explore
an uninhabitable cosmos
petrified us into silence,

but then we burst out laughing
when Gagarin, the first cosmonaut,
dressed in his space suit, waved at us,
peering through his radish-round helmet
gleaming in the terrestrial sunlight
of a Moscow street-parade, as if
the unknown world was to be conquered
by a jolly man with a radish for a head.

1968

Fire torches tonight's dream.
Death seconds fear and molds
a cynical tomorrow. On the news
politicians count bombs falling
over Vietnam and I wish
for a destiny that's mine.

An unknown virus kills a Congo tribe.
All the way here, beneath the Iron Curtain,
I pray for peace on this forbidden Easter.

Will I have children?
Will they have to fear?

This spring in Prague, clandestine
radio stations repeatedly broadcast the last
gasp of a student self-doused in gasoline
burning in protest under Russian rule.

Will I have children?
Will they have to fear tanks
fighting through narrow ancient streets?

Bombs down planes on midsummer flights,
guerrilla has become a multilingual world.
Amid agnostic lives we fight for buried gods
in territories of redemption.

Will I have children?
Will they learn to pray?

My next-door neighbor has discovered hate.
We played the drum of childhood games
and planned for days that were to come.
My night dreams lit to fire when, alone,
I fear the killer taking shape in friends.

Will I have children?
Will they have to die hating,

alone under a mushroom sky?

Que será, será

Que será, será,
Whatever will be, will be ...

Fourteen, in the womb-like warmth
of my mother's house, I listen
to Connie Francis singing the most popular song
of the year. I want to ask the same questions:

What will it be? Who will I be?

The halved breakfast egg and the buttered toast
my mother offers on the dining room table
do not seem to serve as a good metaphor.
"How will my life be?" I ask Mother, but she
rushes me out the door for chemistry class.
"Smile," she says. It's the mantra of the '70s.

Yet I don the melancholic gaze.
The long, thoughtful face of an adolescent
refusing to smile looks back at me
from all the pictures of my youth.

The unknown ahead frightened me,
although I couldn't put it into words.
I wanted to discern the unforeseeable,
but no matter how hard I tried
to peer into that future, I could see
nothing, could imagine nothing.

What will it be? Who will I be?

Now I wish I had taken
the song's words to heart and just let it be,
whatever was going to be, so a few more smiles
could come back to me from the fading
black-and-white past of a charmingly vulnerable
teenage girl whose searching
gaze still questions the future.

Expelled—Bucharest, 1970s

Sometimes during one pop quiz or another,
the loudspeaker exposed the Jew
among our schoolmates, announcing
that some *Popescu* from seventh grade
would now be called *Levy*,
and be expelled from school
for the rest of his life for "high treason."

A big rowdy party usually followed,
complete with music and dancing,
to bid the traitor farewell,
while the neighborhood gossiped
as people do at wakes—
500 American Dollars per capita
of Jew returned to Jerusalem.
Now we were all going to know
someone in the Holy Land.

Nobody had it easy.
I laughed when Ghiury, a Hungarian boy,
mispronounced the name of *The Beloved*
Son of the People, and all three of us
ended up suspended at the school's infirmary.
Ghiury and I for two days, *The Beloved*
framed and hung on the wall, there to keep
a vigilant eye on the delinquent schoolchildren,
until he died, five years later.

One day I was caught writing a poem
about a world hermetically shut,
where I couldn't breathe, couldn't sing, couldn't
speak my mind. Three big men came to school
and asked—"What were you doing in that world,
Comrade?" The new *Even More Beloved
Son of the People*, starched in his frame,
watched me being punished for my latest
delinquency, and wasn't surprised
when the men revealed that I too had
a Jewish grandfather. Although,
I had never known myself to be a Jew,
and as such priced
at 500 American Dollars.

Cinderella

"You shouldn't go to the ball," she says.
"It's not for you. You'd have to have been
born glamorous to fit in with the ball crowd.
You'd have to know how to snub. As it is,
you're too nice, too sweet, too homely …
for a ball, I mean."

I look at her,
my stepmother,
my misfortune, my fate.
Sarcasm shines through
the green glaze of her eyes,
scorn oozes in her words.

"No" she says. "It would be too
adventurous; you'd have to change
into someone else,
the clothes, the dance—
that wouldn't be you."

But I yearn to go,
to defy her malice.
I yearn to change
into a bewitching butterfly,
put on the magical slippers
and dance,

dance, dance
through my epiphany
until dawn.

Grandma's wardrobe

Mid-seventies—Fashion, The Goddess
governing our lives at seventeen, turns "retro"
—meaning the 1930s—mid-calf-length dresses,
minimalist patterns, fluid fabrics, platform shoes,
small purses, demure felt hats with useless
tulle voilettes, modest necklines, glamorous
backless gowns, palazzo pants,
and puffed-up sleeves.

The new vogue had a hint of subtle sexiness,
an open seam, flirty corsages, all in deep blacks,
soft lapis, sunny ambers, garments at once
prudish and coquettish, almost, but not-quite-
clinging to the shapely body, in flowing silks,
sensuous velvets, airy shawls, and soft cashmere.

So much in contrast with the previous years'
daredevil hip-huggers, tie-dyed bell-bottoms,
miniskirts, see-through blouses, frayed short-shorts,
bulky boots, Roman sandals, and flip-flops.

Toni and I were baffled looking at *ELLE*'s pages.
We'll need to revamp entire wardrobes
before summer, just to fit in, we thought. But Toni,
my fashion-savvy friend, perked her head.
Her wistful dark eyes sparkled, and, cheeks aflame,
she said, "Wait! I've got something." And took me
to the attic.

We rummaged through ancient furniture,
disintegrating books, broken toys,
and in a chest of drawers, cherry red,
so dusty our fingers left half-inch-deep prints
while we choked on the powdery past, we found
an *ELLE*-worthy treasure: soft dresses,
leather platform shoes, shawls,
tiny flowery felt hats, gloves, palazzo pants,
and Greta Garbo-style trench coats.
Toni's grandmother's wardrobe.

At seventeen, playing fashion diva with my friend,
I made myself a promise: I too will store my dresses
in an attic someday, so my future granddaughters
can play dress-up, and outsmart
the vagaries of Fashion.

A few baby granddaughters later, and an attic
full of "retro" clothes, I have to put up
with a grumpy husband who nags: "Donate
all those damned old dresses
that don't fit you anymore to the Salvation Army!
Let's turn that useless attic into a workroom,
where I can teach my grandkids
to build model cars and kites."

In my mother's kitchen

"This isn't how
you cut a red onion," she says,
disapproving of my slowness.
"First you need a quick
sharp knife. Watch!"
She halves the curve
of a dark purple onion
into two precise hemispheres.
Flawlessly she strikes
and the rapid rhythm of the blade
goes through, so swift, so clean

there is no time for tears.
In the end, for just an instant,
her layered hemisphere
seems unchanged,
shape held by the inertia
of past wholeness.

It is my turn to cut the other half
while Mother looks at me askance,
but pinned beneath her stare
my hands feel
under the unyielding blade
each severed layer

while I wait
for the inevitable
tear.

Hirosho's new words

At break of dawn he appeared in the village,
saddled with his huge orange backpack.
Jabbering like an exotic bird, he frightened
the women out early in gardens to gather
dew-soaked tomatoes for breakfast.

The fishermen stopped mending their nets,
gaped at him half disbelieving, half bemused
by the sight of a creature so different from any
they'd ever seen, even in movies.

The priest rushed so, he had his priestly robe
inside out when he came to greet the odd man
walking the dusty roads of his parish
before the roosters' first calls. He asked him
who he was, what he wanted.

The good Father tried Latin, Greek,
but neither helped, so he brought Hirosho
to our summer hut, thinking,
townsfolk that we were, we could
find out, in English or French.

Using a map that did not show
our ancient hamlet rising from silky white sand,
Hirosho, the Japanese globetrotter, was lost
on the salt-laced shores of the rugged Black Sea.

We took him in, as the custom was to share
one's bread and one's shelter with a weary
dust-covered traveler. He stayed for a week

in our primitive cottage—no TV,
no indoor plumbing; only a wood-burning stove
in the front room, where we cooked
and spent evenings by the fire.

Every day, villagers came by to look at Hirosho,
make sure he was real, not a fisherman's tall tale.
They asked to see the astonishing stuff he carried
in the backpack: an inflatable bed with a pillow,
a cocoon for a blanket, a floating armchair,
a spider-like net to keep insects away, milk in a can,
a looking-glass no one could shatter,
and matches that lit even when wet.

But mostly they wanted Hirosho to speak.
They listened, faces furrowed in thought,
until a sound made them giggle, exchange
giddy glances, explode into laugher, gleefully
feasting on each other's oddness.

Hirosho's laughter, the villagers thought,
was most wondrous of all—"He laughs
just like us!" they said, shaking their heads
in amazement.

By the third day we taught Hirosho to say
buna ziua, the usual hello, and other
colloquial expressions. There's something
about sharing one's tongue, as if sharing
one's family ties; the bonds that words knit
between us make us kin.

Next morning, on the walk to the beach,
Hirosho said *buna ziua* to every villager,
called them by their names. Some froze
in their tracks, some crossed themselves,
a woman almost fainted by her gate, another
rushed inside scared; but as word of Hirosho's
new speech spread from garden, to stable,
to house, a few fishermen came out
on the street and cheered.

Old Flora, the Medicine Woman,
took Hirosho by the hand,
as one takes a young child,
sat him down on a small wooden bench
by the side of the road,
and asked him to speak, and he did.

She looked him in the eyes, smiling
amidst tears, and said, "You're human,
Hirosho!" and kissed him on both cheeks.

Daily light

Lily, do you remember
how we used to play
in the lake's waters?
Swim to the dark
deep plants
and sleepless fish,
eyes open to find
every sharp rock?

I would dive only
where a tunnel
of light plunged
into the lake, moving
sensual waves
against my body,
knowing when to sink
like an anchor
into the gravel,
when to search
for sun's light
folded heavy with water,
when to find my way back.

The lake kept no memory
of me, no shape, no imprint,
only my footprints
bloomed in the silt
like any other
dark plant, sleepless fish,
for a moment.

I still bathe in the light
diving through tunnels,
looking for ground
to anchor my life,
still wonder why days
keep no memory of me,
no imprint, no shape
only time engraves
blossoms of aging
on my body of clay,

eyes open to watch
for every sharp rock.

Miracles in times of communism

The family on the seventh floor
had so many children
we could never memorize
all their names. We called them
by age order—Big Brother, Twins,
Youngest, Middle, Second to Last,
One in Between.

The neighbors used to whisper
must be a miracle they can all
so much as breathe
in their jam-packed apartment,
a miracle the small loaf of bread
the father brings daily
has enough crumbs
to feed them all.

But one day the father came home
three front teeth missing and a bloody shirt.
Two days later a loud knock on their door
and his wife dressed in black even before
the *duba* carrying him to the precinct
for a last confession disappeared
over a dusty bend in the road.

The day after, the street sergeant
curled his snide lips
and officiously inquired about
a new miracle, asking the Youngest,
"How come your father
ain't being Born Again, again?"

Brâncuşi—November 1974, Romania

We took a slow night train, the three of us,
adolescent girls full of life and grace, bearing
cookies and milk for three big-city boys stranded
under army rule in a poor provincial town—
Brâncuşi's town.

The train station welcomed us with its leftover
pre-war charm mixed in with communist slogans
and Gypsy toddlers, scantily dressed for the winter,
begging.

The main hotel, proletarian mildew smell
& judgmental guises, measured our
"big city" mannerisms and the 18-years-old
emancipation of meeting 3 male friends
in a 3/single-beds hotel room at 8 o'clock
in the morning.

A thick industrial fog covered the world
with the scornful indifference of socialist neglect.
We drifted through the town's cold November
cloaked in sad provincial gray. In the park
where Brâncuşi surrendered to daily usage
the ancestral symbols of his mid-century soul,
workers sat around the *Table of Silence*, laughing
at an old joke, mouths filled with the day's lunch:
bread & salami.

The Gate of the Kiss, shape smoothly caressed
by two sheltered lovers, approved
our since-childhood friendships.
Only the *Infinity Column*, sky-bound,
seemed chaste, majestic, piercing the smog.

We touched the angular shape of *Infinity*'s
rough metal fabric and found it corroded,
permeated by the bankruptcy of gray seeping in
from the train station.

But we were young
and held hands with infinity, laughter,
adolescence & since-childhood friendships.

Fallen patriarch

Grandpa learned to labor at tobacco—
ancestral craft of mystic pleasure,
from his father
and his father's father
on generational fields with no gaps
and no queries.

Stocky fingers in hypnotic movement rolled
chosen leaves speckled with whiskey, mixed
with spices, dried in attics
till the drunken air curled, heavy
with exotic dreams and foggy places. As a boy,
he lit the elders' pipes; at fifteen, he took up
smoking as his given rite of passage.

His youth, like blue smoke, languished thick,
but at the wedding, Grandma put a stop
to burning weeds in pagan bachelor rituals. She,
smart hands and wild reef of beauty,
wove patterns of bequeathed meanings
in wool rugs, blankets, and in children.

She thought smoking was
the devil's chimera. I thought it was hilarious
finding Grandpa, patriarchal stature,
behind the house, in hiding
for our daily puffs of comfort.

Keeping time

We were to meet
under the sooty brass clock
suspended from the ceiling
of the train station, half past five
in the morning, to take the six o'clock express
to a seaside town to watch
a rugby game. I showed up late.
We missed the train.

Your anger, at the boiling point,
dissipated when I explained,
sniffling and embarrassed,
that I hadn't changed my watch
to the country's newly adopted
Daylight Saving Time, and pointed out
that the station hadn't either.
The early-morning train
left us behind to wait for hours.

An old and slothful janitor
carting a rackety green ladder
asked us to help him steady it
on the tiled floor, and he climbed
to the one-hundred-year-old clock
to bring it up to this present of ours.
"Why in God's name should we
mess with it?" he grumbled. "Nothing
good can come of this. Not even time
can escape our meddling anymore!"

Forty years later,
going through the same train station,
we notice the absence of the brass clock.
The place is studded with digital screens
showing time over and over from every
corner of the world. My wristwatch
sets itself up to the right time,
whatever the meridiem, but you never miss
the chance to remind me of the day
we had to take a later train
to the seaside town, and all the way there
we kept repeating the old janitor's words,
laughing at his wisdom, as foolish children do.

Newlyweds

"This can't be! Can't you see? It doesn't fit,
it's the wrong size." He tries again.
The huge hand-carved wood chest won't slide
inside the small niche in my room.
All my white furniture screams
against the dark warmth of this walnut buffet,
a family heirloom, a wedding gift from his mom.

We removed the shelves and books I had there
from long before I knew him. Again he pushes,
jimmies, tries to skid the chest in. Nothing.

The measurements we took were mostly right,
except for the wall's skirting board
and the fancy curvature on the chest's legs
we didn't think to measure.
He finally gives up. Baffled, he looks around—
the piled-up books, the airy, elegant lines
of my furniture bathed in the blue morning light,
while, arms akimbo, tears in my eyes, I don't know
what to do with him, or with his mom's present.
I fear conflict, some hurt that could forever shadow
our lives.

He sighs, moves the bookshelves back, tidies up
the room in silence. I help. Our hands touch,
his brows unfrown, while the quiet despair
on his face turns whimsical, yet his thoughts,
I know, still circle that brown chest
in the middle of a white room, too dark, too big
to fit inside our new life.

Frazzled, I say, "My love, don't worry,
we'll find a place for it."
"I know," he says, amused. "Let's set it
out on the balcony. Agreed?"

A few weeks later a pair of rock doves
built a nest on top of it,
and kept us company for years.

What freedom is

"In the long history of the world, only a few generations
have been granted the role of defending freedom in its hour of
maximum danger."
—J. F. Kennedy (Inaugural Address, 1961)

"While the State exists, there can be no freedom. When
there is freedom there will be no State."
—Vladimir Ilich Lenin (*The State and Revolution*, 1919)

I grew up with Yoshi, the nice Jewish kid
who shared the chewing gum his uncle sent
from the U.S of A. On our sweet-craving
Communist streets, Yoshi doled out
his gum to the neighborhood kids—those he liked
got a fresh half-stick, those he did not
got a pre-chewed lump hygienically washed
with scented Palmolive soap. One day,
in the middle of tenth grade, Yoshi left
to live in the States.

Years later, teaching in an impoverished
mountainous hamlet far from my native town,
I try to convince the country's future shepherds
that we all live free in the twentieth century,
while The Greatest Communist Party on Earth
carries out the Marxist ritual of equal distribution
of wealth—all of which seems to my schoolkids
as fictional as indoor plumbing.

And here comes Yoshi, a tourist
in his native country, eager to see me at my post.
He comes with gifts of soap, and powdered milk,
and coffee for the people in the village, cigars
and gum to please the mayor
and the Politburo chief.

He jokes, raves about New York
the way an Argonaut
would speak of a magical world. Winter
comes with him too—early and harsh. It holds us
hostage in a hamlet where hungry wolves roam
the frozen mud-roads at night and boars rummage
the snow-covered gardens.

Guests inside the mayor's house, we sip red wine
by the fire and chat about the world. "You know,"
Yoshi says, leafing through a dusty
Communist Manifesto he found on a shelf. "Marx
was right—freedom is a bourgeois concept."
"Freedom!" the Politburo chief harangues.
"Freedom from what?"
But our host, not in the mood for metaphysics,
suggests a game of cards, and at midnight,
the Politburo chief wins with an ace of spades.
We rise and toast winter's snow as a good omen
for future fields of golden wheat, corn, grapes,
and then we part as friends.

Days later, after Yoshi's departure
transformed him into a folk hero,

the Politburo chief comes to the school
holding a cigar in his beefy hands.
He looks me in the eye and proclaims
loudly enough for everyone to hear:
"We, the people and the party, think
you are a spy and that Yoshi is your contact
with the West. We have not yet decided
if you committed crimes, but from now on
you will be watched."

"watched!"
howl the stray dogs in the streets
"watched!"
whisper fields of black-eyed Susans
"watched!" say the unreturned phone calls
"watched!"
winks the cheerful Gypsy selling popcorn
"watched!"
screeches a slow train leaving the station
"watched!"
hisses the heavy air tinged with fear,

until this whole twentieth century
feels like a lump of pre-chewed gum, washed
with Palmolive soap, and freedom
equals despair.

Recurring nightmare

I scrape my hand on the swirling leaves
and fleur-de-lis of the wrought-iron gate
trying to find the secret latch. I push
and slither through.

The woolly fog, the poorly lit street,
give me the reprieve I need to escape
the quickening hard footsteps behind me.
I run up the three gray slippery stairs
to the drab entrance door and slink inside.
It's my friend Nona's house. No one is here,
only the stale smell of unkempt furniture
and threadbare rugs.

It is so quiet I can hear the fog
turning to droplets on the windowpanes.
Hiding beside the dusty brocade drapes
I watch the street. The faint gleam
of the slick pavement lessens
the surrounding darkness.

A man in a heavy coat,
a dark, wide-brimmed fedora hat
pulled low over his brows, stops,
looks left, looks right,
shakes hard the locked gate, peers
at the house, mutters a curse,
lights up a cigarette, leaves.

Still, I do not move for a long time; fight
to steady my quick breath; my dress soaked
in my shivering dread, my nails dug deep
into my palms, fearing the Securitate man
who followed me for weeks, all the way

into my dreams, three decades later,
in another life, on a different continent,
even after I have left him behind
in the Old Country.

When it comes to farewells

I leave the massive walnut chest
to my best friend Daria. I mail
the French books and hefty dictionaries
to my high school teacher, retired now
in a provincial town.

I give the ebony wood picture box
to Cousin Mara, let her cling on
to the aged mother-of-pearl arabesque
encrusted on the lid, let her hold dear
the sepia celluloid shadows inside.

To Alex I bequeath the wooden spoon
he made for me in eighth-grade summer camp,
but I keep the red boldfaced almandine
he gave me, sweet crystal witness of our first kiss.

To the emptied rooms—their histrionic poses
and heirlooms much too cumbersome
for packing or giving away, I say *adieu*,
and offer bibelots as keepsakes
to those who come to bid me farewell.

What will I take with me? Truth is,
after years of half-absent glances
and weekly dustings, the ornaments
in my life have so much to say to me
now, that it's time to pack and part.

Tante Lori

She has never been an affectionate aunt,
but knowing how uncertain it is
that she'd see me return from the land
of my exile, she asks me to come
for a last supper.

On the dining room table,
the silver menorah
saved from the Kiev pogrom
Great-grandfather Isaac
escaped reflects the white-laced
tablecloth that survived
Grand-maman Isabelle's house
set on fire by Fascists.

We set the table for two
with the Rosenthal china
left behind by Aunt Irma,
who followed her husband
to America, searching
for gold, a century ago.
I pour the champagne
in the tall crystal flutes
Uncle Andrew did not
take with him when escaping
war and the Red Revolution.

Tante Lori serves celery salad,
beef-stuffed turnips
with spicy horseradish sauce,
and peach pie for dessert.

To avoid sudden tears,
I ask for pie recipes,
cooking secrets, honey
for the tea, and Uncle Paul's
silver teaspoons to stir
the conversation away
from family and faith.

Ubi patria—a prophecy before exile

Because her migrant tribe left, Leana,
the Gypsy we hired to paint our house,
found some other thing to do after
the painting was done, then something else,
'til it was clear she would not leave, so long
as we fed her and paid her, not much pay
for not much work, but still enough
that she could spend Sundays at the corner pub.

Crooked, raspy, full of sharp, bitter curses,
she limped her way through ten pregnancies
and gave one healthy boy to each orphanage
in a thousand-mile radius 'til the State
declared her retarded, and spayed her.
Then she became the best dirge-howler-for-hire
in town. I tell her "shut the hell up
and help with the packing," but it's no use.
"Wheeere are you goooiing?" she wails,
tears grooving her dark cheeks. "Of all people,"
I say, "you should understand!

"You're a Gypsy, you have the call
from afar, the freedom, the mirage,
the road in your blood."
"Do I know roads! Freedom!"
She says like a thespian, "There are *afars*
not even your shadow would follow, roads
that wear you so hollow your bones
change to echoes."

"Stop it!" I say. "I know where I'm going."
"You do? Right off," she says, "your eyes,
your ears will become slanderous witnesses.
No land will seem auspicious harbor,
no water deep enough to cast anchor. A sky,
endless like death, and a slow, deep grave
beneath waves is all your eyes will see.

"You will burn to ashes telling your story
in the barbed-wires of other tongues,
not knowing if your words are a curse
or a prayer, yet you'll never break free
of your lonely language. O! Where you go,
even hunger breaks its neck."

Having left

Leaving
is a matter of suitcases, plane tickets,
farewell parties, and a sudden atmosphere
of drama, when the distance I am becoming
comes into focus in present tense.

Having left
changes the brand-new pair of slippers
Mother packed for my departure
into an absence.

Leaving
turns maps into daydreams about places
that shall soon be greeting me.

Having left
brings a craving so deep I would offer my soul
for Aunt Rada's schnitzels, knowing it would come
with her morose nagging. She remembers me
lighter than leaves, imagines I move
like a swift, shapeless wind in a labyrinth.

Leaving
I take with me notes, addresses,
expect that news of me would be spread
from Mother and Father to cousins and friends.

Having left
I discover how postcards falsify images,
cleanse them of the sounds never heard
and of the smells never smelled elsewhere.

Leaving
I promise a reunion—in a future I dare
plan for.

Having left turns me into a fable
they tell to the young, while I try to keep
those left behind in the same plot
with that which I am becoming.

Back home
they place my framed picture next to an icon
and toast to my health every Sunday, while I
forget their secrets and send them letters
to keep them abreast of the narrative shape
of my days as if a well-kept ledger
were the only way I have to remind them
I am as real as a swift, shapeless wind
in a labyrinth.

Political refugees

for Doiniţa and Mihnea

The locals are kind and help
with food and shelter, just as they did
a generation ago with those
fleeing war and the Nazis.

Official after official asks
about interrogations and threats.
I have to explain wire-tapped phones,
body searches, censored letters,
a country where I am the enemy.

I try to fit the festering past
onto the two inches of white space
allotted on questionnaires,
write my life, tell what would happen if
I were to be sent back, as if white paper
could illustrate the damp dark cells
I would have to share with hunger,
beatings, and the rats waiting for me
in the land of my stories. They tell me

I am free, and don't understand why I can't
stop watching my back at all times, why
I still fear that the hostile government
I'm trying to escape looks over my shoulder,
snatches my thoughts, takes notes, maps
my mind—the only space I have to keep myself
alive.

Roof over far away

He smiles cordially, shuffles papers,
amused by my handwriting—"Typically
European." He's tall, athletic, perfect teeth
and a robust complexion. There is an efficient
nonchalance about him that says *American*.

"You're pregnant?" he asks, over the stack
of questionnaires, letters, applications piled
high on his desk, and I panic—will this mean no
U.S. visa? "That's good." He nods,
slowly examining my medical report, while I
apologize for not knowing English well enough
to put into words why I need to, I have to
go to America, and once there I am going to be
a wage earner, a taxpayer, a charity giver.
And suddenly I want to ask whether,
by a strange coincidence, he knows
what ever happened to Aunt Irma,
who followed her husband to Alaska in 1909.

Her last letter, still safeguarded
in the family album, was sent from Ellis Island.
She writes how embarrassed she felt when a male
doctor weighed, measured, checked her for lice,
looked at her nails and teeth, inspected every orifice
of her body, as if she were some young mare
in the stall.

This land, she writes, *only takes the best of the crop,*
the bold and the healthy: broad-chested men,
good-looking women with strong thighs
and firm muscles, to create a glorious new race.
Yesterday, a philanthropic American woman
came by to give me a fashionable dress
and a shawl, to teach me how to make myself pretty
with perfume, powder, and rouge, to please
my husband and belong.

What ever happened to Aunt Irma? The first
of our good-old-stock to go to the New World,
the one whose calligraphed letter still tells
how eager she was to build a new roof
over a faraway land and never look back.

Immigration

What a wild motley throng we are—
each one of us hauling our one-way luggage
filled to the brim with whatever superstitions
and beliefs we think we'll need to start over
the rest of our lives.

It is a good day for departure—
the autumn equinox. Fate cannot tip the balance
between day and night. The air, ripe with summer,
is clear for flight to the enchanted land where roses
always blossom. How strident our strange tongues
sound inside the airplane, among Americans
returning from vacations.

Just look at us: Ivan nods his head for *no*
and shakes it to say *yes*, in true Bulgarian fashion;
Liuba sings her daughter a sad Lithuanian song;
I hold, as an amulet, a small flute
made of red Carpathian oak;
Imar is clad in his blue African toga.

We are the chosen ones. Why us and not
the others still waiting back on shore? 'Specified
measures, toughening criteria for asylum.[2]'
We have to learn to take whatever chance
brings us, trust our hands, our talismans,
our lucky stars, our freedom.

[2]California Assembly Member Richard Polanco. Assembly Joint Resolution
on Statewide Immigration Impact, 1994

The airplane flies us against time
into a new dawn—a migration in September,
toward *a latter Eden*.[3]

Boisterous, Imar strikes up a conversation
with a maternal-looking lady from Kentucky.
"You American?" he asks. "I American too,"
he says. "In five years I American. Go work,
pay tax, get rich, be free," he chants,
drunk with the music of his new tongue.

Loud and passionate like any pilgrims,
we leave our seats to crowd a window,
when Liuba calls: "There, there She is!"

The Mother of Exiles[4]—the statue,
and her golden flame brightening
the shores of our promised land. Each one of us,
homeless, tired, poor, come to offer our sole
possession—our future.

[3]"Unguarded Gates," by Thomas Bailey Aldrich
[4]"The New Colossus," by Emma Lazarus

Emigrants

for Şerban and Alin

We're nearly there, my love.
In a few hours all that we know
of the world will become
an eerie country. Behind us
the Iron Curtain, ahead—
a land where no one expects us.

Inside my womb a wing-like beat;
our child makes known his presence.
There is no angry sea to part,
no Bethlehem waiting in the dark,
no stable, no magi, no guiding star.
We are a man, a woman,
and an unborn child in search
of something intangible,
of freedom.

Our son will never understand
how terror could be hidden
in common things, he'll never
be afraid to think, to speak
his mind, he'll never know
grandparents and traditions.

His myth starts now, with our flight.

Immigrant

It turns out my childhood hobby,
collecting postcards, is now getting in the way.
In the past, everything I knew about this place
I knew from postcards.

What wasn't pictured was half-guessed,
smells assumed, metal and glass textures
imagined, musical church bells filling the air,
presumed. I used to see myself walking
within the images, strolling in the park,
chatting with neighbors in grocery stores,
joking with coworkers by the water fountain.

Now I try to inhabit my postcard by becoming
its clandestine language; mimicking accents,
intuitive syntax, wishing my half-known words
could help me understand the rough edges
of the city's sounds. Inside this *postcard*,
when I ask for directions, my accent
makes a schoolgirl suspicious; on the stairs
to the subway, the rushing mob accuses me
of walking too slow.

My humor becomes the first casualty of translation.
The city's pulse sounds like a sermon in exile—
there's nothing familiar around. I can't distinguish
a smile from a sneer. Life is measured differently.
Time is told backwards.

Each day I become an incoherent story
where my past—what makes me tangible, real—
fades away. Had I never imagined this place
I wouldn't struggle now to make of it something
I could recognize; a clear picture

in which silhouettes don't superimpose one another,
hazy atop blurred patches of color
mocking the outline of neighboring objects,
while the oil-laced water puddles on the sidewalk
mirror my journey.

New York, New York (1990s)

for Filip

From my suburban distance it looks almost serene.
A floating star. Adorned oriental jewel.
Between river and ocean, endless shades of blue
encapsulate New York in a placenta of dense
water and sky. Sunset-forged windows,
pointed roofs; the skyline confesses
to an architectural marathon: exquisite,
steeliest, glassiest, wealthiest, tallest,
extreme and limitless. Up close
the puzzle reveals broken successions,
unsettled meanings, traffic, faces, gestures,
stories—too many to listen to, too fast
to understand.

The city
accommodates description
in the context of a new English language
with unrelated accents, exotic dialects,
translated identities, large streets dwarfed
by even larger buildings.

On 42nd
a bag lady bargains poems—
one dollar per incoherent bit of wisdom
hand-calligraphed on parchment paper.
Along quarrels of territorial graffiti someone
sells grass and hypnotic illusions.
Next door to a peep theater (show in progress),
a Baptist minister, athletic under ceremonial cloth,

preaches in Afro-urban rhythm
against a futile world—
ours,
while above him
a cardboard Mickey Mouse
sermons us all on the compulsive
need for advertising.

On the issue of a parking ticket,
two hurried nuns jump-starting their Toyota
implore a handsome cop
for human understanding.

Tourists,
amused by their own confusion,
proudly make use of foreign
inflections to buy all-beef hotdogs
from Hindu vendors.

A rabbi
sporting centuries-old fashion
consults his beeper to find out who last
inquired for the Messiah.

Elusive Orion,
a replica of modern Homer, greets
visitors at MoMA with schizophrenic urban fables.

On Fifth,
a siren-blazing ambulance gets stuck,
on Madison
a fire truck stops traffic,
on Wall Street
a businessman, fearless pedestrian
of his current fate, hunts dollars and ignores
a screeching yellow taxi,
and part of the endemic noise
church bells call to cleansing evening ritual.
Inside St. Patrick's, a parishioner's cell phone
punctuates the celestial "Ave Maria."

The entire human race
hurries through town, preoccupied
with justifying its own struggle; to get a paycheck,
to discover treasures, to find a well-paid notoriety
and, if all else fails, to make it from the city
to suburbia.

Almighty Dollar, the addictive god,
laces Uptown, Midtown, Downtown, Chinatown,
and levitates from subterranean hurry
through roasted pretzels, grounded steam ghosts,
and sugar-coated peanuts, while Donald Trump
trumpets his wealth, and royal heirs
go jogging incognito among purpose-driven runners
in the park, enslaved by newly reinstated
health edicts, courtesy of a Roman era.

Inhabitants of Greenwich Village,
shaped into abstract canvas, lustrous celebrities
from Broadway, psychotic homeless,
stalking paparazzi, Italians
selling ethnic pride in pizza, young Asian gangsters
hiding pistols under dragon masks, all
parrot mercantile ideologies of freedom
and loftily exercise the right to eat
delivered Chinese rice.

On Harlem's pavement, a black man
sleeps off his freedom; close by, an older woman
learns to read Help Wanted ads. Policemen
on horseback keep at bay humane protesters armed
with makeshift blades, while furred
and glittered socialites applaud
a country-music concert.

And above all, uninterrupted,
a headline-belted building lists last hour's wars,
national deficit, Olympic champions,
epidemic hunger, record
nor'easter season over the Atlantic.

Yet, from a distance, it does look tapestry-like
reiteration of a Renaissance dream
of fantastic richness
and an incomprehensible future.

The prodigal son

Every day my thoughts go back
as if looking for a measure
of approval: a brother's
pat on the back, a father's nod
for how I've spent my days—
rise early to seed the new land,
say prayers in the old tongue
to keep them pure, do a good deed.

At home they wonder if I
get old like they do, while I
keep them faultless in my mind,
cleansed of their ills, and I forget
their sins as I want them
to forgive me my absence.

I know they're waiting back there,
right where I left them; ready
to settle their anger, flaunt
their trust, offer a sign of their love.

Back there they twist the fragmented
news they receive about me into a parable
mirroring my past habits, their memories
of me—the adventurer, the jester,
the careless dreamer,

while like a pilgrim I try to keep sacred
the old creed of my tribe,
even if the price of it
is hunger.

Baby and Child Care

for Alin

A wrinkle between almost invisible eyebrows;
you frown in your sleep. I have no one
here to tell me what to do, how to love you,
how to care for you, only books by Dr. Spock
on the nightstand—an old translation Father
sent and the newest English-language edition.

Many things do not match anymore.
The older book stained with grits,
gives potion recipes, breastfeeding advice.
The new book, still smelling of fresh ink,
mentions brands of formula milk, ready-made
ointments, disposable diapers.

Oh, the hours I spent as a little girl swaddling
dolls in cloth diapers! Mother or Aunt Rada
would show me again and again the proper way
to fold and tuck the soft cloth. Their hands so smart!
My own hands clumsy, I feared I'd never be
a good mother.

Now you're here. Your miniature toes,
your fingers curled in a small velvet fist.
Now, the diaper part is easy. Mother
and Aunt Rada sent long letters,
wise advice about feeding, discipline,
but none of it matches your hunger,
the formula, the order of life

in the new American edition
of *Baby and Child Care*, and I have no one
here to teach me a lullaby. You sigh
in your sleep. When you wake up
you'll look at me, trusting I know how
to fold and swaddle the world, give it to you
just right for your fingers to grasp.
And I can't read English well enough
to find a lullaby Dr. Spock
might have added to his new book.

You open your eyes, search for my face.
I start singing the only song I know,
about a mother and a child, alone,
one dark winter night.

Learning Essential English

Fresh off the boat
my vocabulary consisted only of: *doors, love,*
story, bridge, trouble, water. Praise the TV,
the radio, the pursed-mouthed WASP librarian
who, as if under duress, handed me the book
Essential English, Lessons for Beginners.
Bless PBS, *Sesame Street*, Mister Rogers,
and my kid, who helped me acquire
Language Skills!

My tot and I learned to speak at the same time.
We mimicked Mister Rogers, exercised sounds,
syllables, words, until I put on the thin veneer
of grammar needed to count money in a bank.
I was ready for the workplace in West New York,
NJ, where coworkers and customers alike
palavered all day long in Cuban-tinted Spanish.

But English was the language of my new land
and I had to conquer it or perish.

One evening, Sylvia, my kid's babysitter,
an old *Yiddishe mama*, a great lady,
sat me at her table and asked: "Do you, at home,
still speak Romanian to the kid?" I told her
that I did. "Don't!" she demanded.
But how could I not? I didn't yet know
how to play, to caress in my new tongue;
besides, the tyke was soaking up both
English and Romanian all at once.

"Well, then," she said, a bit annoyed.
"Is there a word in your Romanian
that sounds like ... you know ... our
four-letter word?" I didn't understand.
"You know the word, don't you?"
My *Sesame Street* vocabulary was bulging
with four-letter words, but somehow I sensed
she was trying for one I hadn't heard.
"That ... word," she said, signaling
something perplexing with her hands.
I said: "Pardon me, Madam, my fault. I don't."

She got up and walked around the room,
nervously picking up toys strewn
over the carpet. The kids edged closer,
stared at me as if I were the bearded lady
in a freak show.

"Well," she retorted. "The word F-U-C-K?"
But spelling was for me a foreign concept.
"*Efyousikay?*" I mimicked her.
"Yes! Do you have a word that sounds like it?"
"No. Why?"
"Your son says it all the time."
"Ah," I said. "What does it mean?"
"What do you mean, what does it mean?"
Apologizing once again I whispered
"What is *efyousikay?*"

She slapped her forehead, realizing
I had mistaken the spelling for the word.
"That's not it!"

A travel guide.
In my purse I kept a travel guide.
I reached for it, but she groused,
"No, it is not a travel-guide
kind of word." That information,
and the crimson color of her face,
gave me a hint, but which one,
and how should it sound,
since it was clear that *efyousikay*
was not it?

She leaned over the table, very close
to my face, and said, "Is there a word
in your Romanian that sounds like *fuck?*"
"Oh, yes! Yes! Yes! *To do, to make*."
Indignant, she pointed to my son.
"He says it all the time! To Lisa and to Nathan—
'Let's *efyousikay* a castle'"
"Oh," I said. "What does it mean?"
"Well, you know ... it means ..." she said,
weaving her hands, kneading the air.
"… with a man ..." It was my turn to gasp
"Oh my. *Efyousikay!*"

Cultural differences

Maybe because our children are young,
Thanksgiving, this American holiday,
is a time to celebrate how we made our own path
once we left our parents.

My hosts perform a dance of euphemisms
to avoid long-past quarrels, for holiday's sake.
Nothing unusual, just the stuff of everyday life
they reenact, as turkey and sweet potatoes
are passed around, children's faces wiped,
old parents helped with the seating, wine served,
thanks given.

Lisa recalls her father scolding her after a march
on Park Ave. Her favorite peace pin is still visible,
now on her child's teddy bear. Marjorie begins
the story of shopping with Mom—a shirt she never
wanted, yet she still keeps in its original wrapping,
price tag intact. I watch them going in and out
of their pasts: taking the school bus on Sixth Ave.,
bargaining their way through adolescence,
Sixties protests, Village flea markets. For them,
each step through life had an unhurried stride,
the instinct of willed paths. I want to tell
of my childhood in that alien country
they know nothing about.

There was no thanks-giving, no sweet potatoes.
Haggling my adolescence through irascible
family dinners meant keeping peace pins
hidden from the spying eyes of a father

suspected to be the political enemy,
while wine and fear-silenced protest
was passed around.

I wish I could tell of a time when there was
a bequeathed path, an unwanted shirt,
a future intuitively known. I start my story
with a simple introduction: the landscape,
the streets, the interdictions, the customs,
the usual stuff of life—weddings, baptism,
departures, and how all of it had to be
hinted at in gestures to avoid mentioning
church, exiled uncles, or political protest,
for our freedom's sake.

In the end, it all becomes so complicated.
The background swallows the story
as I get lost explaining why there were no
flea markets, no school buses, no baptism,
not even price tags or wrapping paper,
only secretly kept peace signs
and clandestine protests so dangerous
it poisoned the air of my family dinners.

They stare at me when I tell of my past
as if I'm speaking of a fictional character,
while I need to be taught, like a young child,
of thanks-giving, of simple strides
through a fear-free life, and be forgiven
when spilling once more the bitter wine
of my alien past.

Jesus on the sidewalk

Summer.

Noon offers no shadows,
no double meanings, nothing oblique.
The sun-bleached town
forfeits tri-dimensionality.

Seven-year-old Jesus, mother illegally
waiting on tables at the diner, father
increasingly drunk, doodles the sidewalk
in white chalk.

A suit-and-tie man rushes out
of City Hall. Chilled like a melon,
he smiles cordially through reforms—
welfare, taxes, minimum wages.
"Do you like the desert summer, Jesus?"
"You should try the New York blizzard,"
says Jesus. "Last winter, before we came here."

Jesus sings to himself out of tune
about tomorrow, and someone's love
moving west, and the all-around world.
"Always going west, we end up coming
back from the East," he sings to himself.

The chalk is dust now. We all regain
some shadow, oblique aureole
of a shortly-past-noon sun going west
over shelterless Jesus, mother illegally
working at the diner.

Old 9W

to Alin

Child,
I watch you shuffle
the copper foliage
of this suburban forest
slowly reclaiming Old 9W.

The glorious interstate
domesticated
to a promenade
is doomed
by the eroding Palisades
and by a forest
urbanized into green acres.

You are too young
to be held hostage
by the bittersweet wisdom
of fallen leaves, of aging.
You just blink
when migratory storks pass us by.

Mother tongue

Mom, you complain
a foreign accent
lurks in my words,
a strange orthography
takes root in my letters,
and my speech often turns
into a tangle of tongues.

I can't offer any excuse.
I just live
between two languages,
in a space
I hardly understand,
where logic and grammar
no longer tame the words
displaced by translation.

Sometimes I fail to feel
where the native tongue ends,
where the foreign one begins.
I walk in and out of languages,
trying to hold on to what is alien
to all: a space un-spelled,
clear of words;
a space that, like intuition,
escapes any narrative,
where thoughts pulse shapeless,
clamorous, vital, indifferent
to any alphabet;

a space where I face
the cunning betrayal
inherent in all tongues,
the incompleteness of words,
their dyslexic attempt
at description.

But, my dearest, don't worry.
Although there is only one word
for love in this foreign language
I still live all the seven words
I taste with my mother tongue.

Picture for America

Next to me in the subway,
two women speaking a Nordic dialect
study a photo greeting-card. A family,
dressed up in their Easter best, smiles back.
Teary-eyed, the older of the two
points to the teenage boy in the center
of the picture, showing off a droll pose—
left index finger at his temple,
as if in deep thought.

I used to be part of family
greeting photos too. A group of us:
mother, an aunt or two, a few cousins—
whoever showed up for the occasion,
would sit for a picture to be sent
to an uncle gone to America.
I'd be dolled up in my best clothes, poised,
determined to prove to those who left
that we were as glamorous,
as well-dressed, as smart, as alive
as the ones they saw every day.

So much I did not grasp back then!
I did not see how the picture revealed
the teenage girl was no longer the baby
left behind, how odd it was to see
Aunt Nelly still dressed like a hippie.

I did not know the glossy image
could not hide the resignation
in Mother's smile, the gray hairs
at Father's temples, and the peach tree
in the background,

same peach tree as in all the old pictures;
familiar, unfolding its blossomed limbs
toward all of us, as if for an embrace.

Naturalization

Like a bird after crossing an ocean
still knows how to build a new nest,
like a seed blown to a foreign soil
remembers to grow its flowers,
I had to become part of my new land,
let go of what I knew of myself,
change how I count, multiply, divide.
I had to understand sweet potatoes,
show my feelings in a tempered way,
teach my tongue the diplomacy
of bizarre expressions, discipline
my gestures to fit strange customs,
so I could be accepted in the order
of this new life as not too alien
a blossom.

It wasn't a skin I shed, but one I tore off
with my own hands, all the while asking,
why can't I, like a severed muckworm,
heal and go on, oblivious to the other self?
Why can't I, like a hermit crab,
inhabit whatever space a shell offers?
My old self, a nearsighted god,
haunted me, while my plumage burned
and I knew I'd never again be
of a place, of a tribe; only of a mourning,
a prayer, a loss. But it is hard to live
without any identity.

Every day an unexpected noise
coming like a musical note
from the new leaves speaks
of the future. To decipher it
is to stitch a kind of intimacy
with the world, with the order
and the secrets of hunger,
with the slow cellular life
growing beneath the skin.

And then,

one day comes like a hallelujah—
the sun rises at the edge of a calm sea
pulling and pushing sediments of the past,
residues of beliefs, the thirst for survival.

Life turns into mythology sometimes.
How else could I have risen again
had I not first burned like a common bird?

Legend of bread

Yeast melting in warm milk,
lemon zest, vanilla beans,
a spoonful of spiced Cuban rum
and the entire kitchen fills
with the aroma of egg yolks
golden-whipped with sugar and spices,
until the air, baptized
with the scent of raisins and walnuts,
rises against the darkening day.

Outside, the snow stifles the garden,
bends the evergreens,
while my son, no longer a child,
restlessly shovels to free a walk-path
away from the house.

I'll bake for him
the sweet holy bread
my mother used to bake
back in the land of my childhood.

When he comes in,
tall, hardened by winter,
the subtle sweet-scent of this cooking
will make him say, just as I used to say,

the house smells of bread,
the house smells of home.

My father's tomatoes

He knew the law but didn't care.
He wanted his heirloom tomatoes
grown from seeds smuggled in
from his father's garden
in the Old Country—yellow, orange, red,
misshapen or perfectly spherical,
sweet and fragrant, like childhood.

He filled up a few socks,
wrapped them up in newspapers
hid among shirts, ties, soap bars,
and managed to land with them
in New York without
being sniffed out by patrol dogs
at the airport.

"Where will you grow them?" I asked,
incredulous when he held up
the seed-filled socks like trophies.
"Right here," he said triumphantly,
"on the terrace. You'll see, come March
I'll plant them in pots, care for them
all spring, and by August we'll eat a salad
like you haven't had since the feasts
we had in Grandpa's garden."

Around us February laced the roofs
with icicles, dirty snow covered
the sidewalks, and the elevated train
rattled the windows, speeding by so close
I could see the passengers inside.

But spring was sure to come;
the nearby trees
showed off their swollen buds,
and by summer,
my father's stowaway tomatoes,
red, yellow, orange, thin-skinned
and as fragrant
as they used to be, became
part of Brooklyn's cityscape,
quite visible from the windows
of elevated trains
passing by.

Navajo Rug

for Mother

One day, after I ran away from home,
after the woven guilt of what I had
once said or done had faded,
I went to buy an oriental rug
from an Armenian
with eyes dipped in honey
and rugs telling fables
the world over.
I chose one
to go with my new country,
thick like bluegrass
and chiming the earthly colors
of Navajo stories.

I took it to my new house
like a bridegroom takes a bride
and lay it down on the wood floor.
The dusk's light coming through the windows
gave depth to the sandy background,
and to the blues and pinks
of the geometric flowers.

My children flung their baseball hats,
their kites, their hurried gazes
over my new rug
and said, "It's nice;
it looks like the Romanian one
Grandma has in her bedroom,

back
where you grew up."
And suddenly I noticed
the patterns, the symmetry,
the diamond shapes, the jagged lines,
the arrows, the eyes.
A peasant in my Eastern country,
a Navajo weaver in my Western one
have entwined the universal myth
I needed
like a wedding needs a bride.

The fig tree

Our small garden grows
on the rough face of a stony hill,
rooted more in gravel than in soil. Here,
summers are too hot, springs too wet,
and in winters, nor'easters stumble old trees
to the ground and blow thick sheets of ice
and snowdrifts on the land.
Gardens on these slopes survive
only by the grace of God.

And though we do take pride in owning
a lush lawn, plant native rhododendron,
sycamore, and sassafras, we dare not seed
any exotic flowers, for fear we wouldn't know
how to take care of life foreign to this land.

Only Joe, our neighbor, brought a fig tree
from Italy, where he fought when young,
during the Second World War.

The fig tree grew into a fruitless bush,
survived through alien land covered in rags
each winter wrapped safe by Joe, as if it were
a present, or his youth kept whole, away
from shrapnel-pierced memories of battles.

A slice of earth

Last night, when I caressed the tulip tree
growing in my garden, its wrinkled bark
stirred from the world beneath my skin
the rough hands of a gardener. Granddad,
I dreamed of you last night. You knew
how to bend the stubborn soil
into full and fragrant harvests of peonies,
lilacs, roses, or the simplest of lilies.

Unlike you, I was a city dweller.
For me flowers were accessories
to living rooms and birthdays as bouquets,
or window boxes.

At the outskirts of town your hands
holding rich clumps of clay were stilled
before I cared to learn how to wed bulbs
to soil, how to grow roots.

Now it is my turn to find a slice of earth to lay
my shadow on, to own what grows on it, to break
and plant a stubborn soil, make a garden of my own
and dream of roots.

Birth of a garden

We come inside after tilling and hoeing
the arid ground of our parched garden.
Tired and careless, we wipe our foreheads
with earth-stained hands, and in so doing
we become baptized into gods
whose wishes will decide which plant shall die
and which shall be granted the right to thrive.

Past owners of this land have allowed
ivy to grow wild and greedy. Strong vines
took over spots where, long ago, hortensias
and sage bloomed. But the ivy climbed
its chaotic will for life over young evergreens,
and loop by loop the stubborn stems stifled
all that could have been.

We had to fight the ivy shoot by shoot.
You pulled its main, I cut its veins. It bled
on our bruised and blistered hands. Yet, sore,
we grieved and bemoaned this sacrifice but did
uncover worms, rodents' nests, and the earth
locked powerless beneath.

Our children, sweaty, sunburned, kept vigil
to the line up to where ivy would be allowed
to hedge around the land. We labored, fought,
conquered a garden. And now it's time
to pray for rain and mild weather, lament
the ivy we had to cut so that spring
could bloom its many shades of life. We pray,
knowing we did as right as we knew how.

Going home

"Come!"
they said, "the witch is dead,
the tyrant gone, your deeds forgotten,
and freedom blossoms like sweet poppies
in a wheat field. Come, come,
come home, we miss you!"

In my mind, for so long
I circled alone, like a hawk
without a nest, above the place
I left behind, returning there
endlessly, traveling
imaginary roads. I lived
in the present,
planning the future,
yet obsessing
over forgotten names and places,
wondering if it was
a memory lapse or a deeper
forgetting.

The past was what I was losing
and needed to find again.
I listened
to the oracular divination
implied in the plea.
I came.

I came
to rediscover tribal gods
and collect various blessings;

to find the wool sweater I left
unfinished, still speared to the spool
of yarn with the same knitting needles.

I came
to a world of aunts and cousins
humming a long-longed-for song,
to the wine-soaked conversations
past midnight when the moon pales
with fright deciphering
the cry of a lonely owl;

I came
to wild dances and dove calls
at sunrise, to all the rococo
excesses of my youth.

I came
to fill my lungs
with the Black Sea's salty air;
to find the treasures lost
under dusk-tinted skies—
fragments of life I scattered
on this shore; the sour cherries'
succulent aroma.

I came
expecting my old slippers
waiting dusty by the door
and a score of restless nephews
and nieces I had only seen in photos.

I came
to Mother and her gardenia-fragrant hugs
and to see once more the deep sigh
in my father's eyes, and the garden,
and the poplars, and the five
whispering willows by the lake.

I came to saunter once again
on the linden-lined streets
of my native town, back
to that one feeling
I have craved—
to be home.

I came.

Mother and daughter

Somewhere in the house I can hear
the melodious clink of china
and silverware.

It is a day like the days I remember
from childhood: a Friday,
the color of forget-me-nots.
Framed by the soft folds of red velvet drapes,
the overgrown garden outside comes in
through the windows. The cuckoo's quavering cry
echoes from the tall grass, and roses climb
on the arched limestone portal.
An unusually oblong-shaped sun reminds me—
today I will walk in my old footsteps.

Mother comes into the room with a breakfast tray—
chai, homemade jam from last year's mulberries,
and dark, thick-crusted bread risen
from crushed grains, smelling of walnuts
and wildflowers.

Breakfast in bed, what a treat!
To see her slender hands reflected
on the gold-rimmed white china and hear her
retell the old story of the mulberry tree
Grandpa planted the day of my birth.
"Every adoration deserves a monument,"
he said. We chant his words, resurrecting his voice
for a second, while quick tears fill our eyes.

"You know, the mulberry," Mother sighs,
"is almost dry. Only a few branches gave fruit
this year." Then, looking at the neglected gazebo
crumbling in the garden, she asks, "Where you live
now, do people die of the same ills as we do here?"

We fall silent. But, just as in the past,
our silence has its own rules.
It moves through the framed pictures
and knickknacks on the bookshelves, reacts
with the fading red-colored Bukhara rug
on the floor, until it changes
into another element—anger, or exhaustion,
and the air, like an old ghost, recounts
a long-ago conversation that has since turned
into something solid—dust on windowpanes,
or on the ceiling, where, in one corner,
a ladybug caught in a spider's web
offers a decorous death.

Immortals

They keep confronting me
when least expected. In a drawer,
where Mother keeps her Alzheimer's
medicine, the psychedelic ring
of my first flower-girl engagement suddenly
shows up, as if from a well, a womb
of things immortal, those I cannot get rid of.

What can be done with what remains immortal—
gods, fetishes, totems, even a superstition,
your own recollections? Kill them? Imagine
confessing to a cruel fantasy: slaying
the Tooth Fairy for having believed in her
for too long, or my gossiping aunt who authored
a legend around my teenage years' infatuation
with a cousin. What's to be done? Lose them;
as it happens with notebooks in trains, or raincoats
forgotten in airports?

Lost—the gods, the sacred totems, the rings,
the love notes would cease to be any part of me,
just like the lucky underwear I wore religiously
for finals in college succumbed to wear and tear.
Imagine! All the immortals I keep as symbols
of my own infallibility, lost at some moving.

Slowly, their memory would fade away. No guilt,
no bloody scene to remember, not the tearful
drama of having to say, "It's over!"
Only the knowledge that I lost something,
and if I knew where I'd go retrieve it. A simple

inward lie, a postponement of immortality
until (if ever) it becomes convenient
to recall them, like the nickname I gave
my pacifier became a sign of my precocity
after I safely turned forty-five.

Or maybe I should just nudge all Immortals
out of sight, as I did with poor Sisyphus
when I stopped considering defiance
the only acceptable lifestyle. He's still
pushing some boulder all the way to the top
of that jagged mountain, but seems remote now,
when, whatever he did to deserve
such a punishment, I'm no longer part of it.

The storyteller

for Coca

Would you look at me
with the same glee if I told you
that each harvest, plucking lemons
in my own orchard made me weigh not
the strong citric scent
of the dark green leaves, or the fruits
larger than any "jumbo size" we could find
in our wintry country, but the need for chai,
for its warmth—the fragrant steam-ghost
of a dried flower from a long-past summer
you could hold in your mouth
to chase away morning chills?

Would your eyes light up
with the same awe if I told you
that Halloween, this peculiar feast
honoring resurrection's sinister faces,
made me hunger for the way
we used to celebrate Easter Eve
with its sorrowful songs, its solemn
cortege of candles carried through streets
into a pilgrimage of light?

Would your voice fill
with the same wonder if I told you
that on a lofty canyon, surrounded
by the angular geology of telluric heights
cloaked in solitude, I thought

of our thick-forested mountains,
their human shapes,
their reachable summits,
the many signs of travelers?

Would you still be proud
of me and my many languages
if I told you that, while speaking them fluently,
all I want
is to curse in my native tongue and be
understood?

Sour-cherry pastries

for Mihaela

The gate to your garden still squeaks the loud *ti-do*,
there still is a wooden bench
under the sour-cherry tree, and blossoming roses.
I thought fifteen years would have been
long enough time to forget landscape, details.

The sun, an upturned honey jar, glazes the day
as it did each July. Your mom comes to the door
wearing one of her festive aprons; only, this time,
her kind eyes are teary, her fingers knobby.
She thanks God for having the chance to see me
once more, as if I were her long-lost daughter,
not your schoolmate. Fifteen years is enough time
to get old.

We sit at the table
under the young sour-cherry tree planted
after I left to replace the one knocked down
in a storm. Your mother brings pastries,
my favorites, and apologizes for not being able
to make them like before. "Can't knead
as much ... arthritis," she says. I look at her
and try to guess which age left what mark
on her slight body.

Alone, we scrutinize each other.
You have cut short your blond curls,
my waistline has thickened a bit,
our voices have ripened.

Yet, we can still laugh—
loud like unbridled adolescents.
The ebullience of shared gossip
still brings tears of joy. "No, no, no,"
you shout. "Sandy put the plate on the bed.
Don't you remember? We were
already playing when Theo showed up."

"No!" I say. "You forgot how clumsy he was.
We were playing cards and that's why
he put the plate on the bed, to make room
on the table. Only, afterward, absentmindedly,
he sat on the bed, right on top
of all the sour-cherry pastries. Oh God,
how we screamed! Schnauzy, the dog,
leaped up at Theo's butt to lick the custard,
and you couldn't stop laughing for so long,
I was afraid you were going to choke.
Theo, poor soul, was embarrassed to tears!"
"Yes, yes, he was crying!"

Above our heads, the sour-cherry tree whispers
a blessing of cool breeze. The pastries
your mom baked for my return taste as fragrant
as the ones her younger hands used to make,
and for once I don't have to pretend—it feels good
to be back.

Feta cheese and tomatoes

for Mininina

Beneath striped awnings
and sun-faded umbrellas,
among peasants' high-pitched calls,
housewives' insistent bargaining,
merchants' cunning laughter,
and barefooted Gypsy beggars,
the red and plump fragrance
of tomatoes fills an iridescent
open market.

They are as big
as I remember them.
Thin-skinned and heavy
with lush flavor—almost sweet.
"Only a few coins a kilo,"
a young man proclaims,
pushing his barrel with red
and orange tomatoes to a stand.

"And here's some feta cheese
for you to taste," his wife cajoles,
offering a slice of the whitest cheese
still dripping with brine.

Instinctively, I say,
"Give me a kilo each."

Tilting her head as if to find
a clearer light, the young woman
looks at me while wrapping
a large cube of cheese
and a few huge tomatoes
and slowly says: "You're not
from around here."

How does she know?
I didn't bargain? Is the kilo
not the usual measure anymore?

Taking my bag I realize
I have forgotten
how heavy kilos feel,
and, slanting my own head
like she does, I tell her
how long a time it's been
since I last bought
a kilo of tomatoes,
and then I pay the price.

Plan a small family reunion—a reliable group

Be prepared to expose/hear/see/be called out
on everything. Any part of your past may resurface.

Don't be surprised if in your absence some
have grown a beard, do not flinch when learning
the names they have given to their newborns,
or how they are disciplining their young.

Nobody here expects your opinion,
and they've long since lost the habit
of asking you for advice. Don't worry
when each one of them coming to greet
your return wants to bid you farewell,
knowing you are just a traveler,
used to strange spices, readily twisting
your tongue into foreign-sounding words.

Go through the obstacle course
of their questions about your life over there,
through their stubborn rhetoric about roots,
land, ancestry, without mentioning
how none of it matters nowadays. They know
you have saved what was needed,
even if that is less than a ghost. They know
the mythic world of a Carpathian forest
still whispers its magic inside you,
and the Black Sea still pulses its salt
under your skin. They know, even below
the charred ground of your exile,
you have grown slow, intricate roots
that carry the flower of their kin.

Don't be upset when they recite proverbs
telling how the earth's grit and gravel
may never lie lightly on you, and how your grave
will never know your past. They don't mean
any harm; they're just angered by how much
they missed you, and how little of it
can be put into words. This is your family
gathered to honor your return. Don't try to explain
how your life story could be equally made to fit
contrary parables—freedom or longing, vagabond
or adventurer. Let them say what your absence
felt like to those departed; after all, this return
is not the end of your journey.

Aunt Rada's schnitzel

They all come—aunts, uncles, cousins.
Some have grown, others have shrunk.
Even the departed show themselves
in the fresh faces of the young, in the voices,
the gestures—inherited like the family stories.

They bring sweets and flowers to celebrate
my return. The table is set,
and on the damask tablecloth,
white china flaunts its world of perfect roses.

I meet and salute each one of them
with a litany of words
rather than the usual greetings.
At first they seem to recognize my footsteps,
my voice, and, hungry as I am, I take their hugs
as a welcoming feast, until a young niece
who looks like our late Tante Lori, says,
"We don't say *swell* anymore, and if I were to hold
my fork the way you do, Mommy would say
I have no manners." Suddenly, everyone notices
I use old-fashioned expressions, I follow
obsolete customs, familiar,
yet from a different time.

To save the conversation, Aunt Rada says,
"I never knew my schnitzels
were your favorite food. Of course, you know,
I had to change the recipe; we're careful
with our cholesterol here too."

From the starched tablecloth a knife
shines its sharpness and Uncle Alex
passes on the tomato salad, while I feel
I have to readjust my size to the new
measurements of a foreign land,
my currency to a different coin. Again.
And silently I chew my food.

But it must have been a strange year
for tomatoes; they don't taste
the way I remember them, or maybe
my memory, like a cryptic oracle, promised
I could paddle the same waters twice,
and I believed.

Turning over in his grave

The taxi driver jerks his head
toward the house, asking, "Whaddya you think,
ma'am, is he turning over in his grave
for what's become of us?"

The driver figures I am old enough to know
what he's talking about. Stuck in lunch-hour traffic
this sunny May Day, we're idling
in front of Ceaușescu's villa. Closely guarded,
thirty years after his execution, there is no sign
to tell what the house is being used for nowadays.

"I'm sure he is," the driver goes on,
scrutinizing my reaction in the rearview mirror.
"He must be," I say tentatively, poker face on,
not knowing which of the 'popular' divides
my driver stands on, but feeling captive for the ride.
The car's radio, set on a religious station, bellows
a lengthy apocalyptic sermon. On the dashboard,
icons and crosses sway with Christian piety
at every turn; window stickers attest,
as per regulation, the new taxi is privately owned.
"How could he not," the driver says, "seeing what
these idiots made of his beloved country!"

The traffic thins a bit, we're slowly rolling.
He goes on. "When he was president, we were
debt-free and now the deficit is killing us! Yeah,
we couldn't talk freely, nobody was allowed
to own a business, or so I'm told.

I was only knee-high back then,
but all the sob stories about the hard life,
freezing to death in poorly heated houses,
famine, the Securitatea beating people
for no reason, are much exaggerated,
aren't they, ma'am?" He glances back.

"How old were you in '89?" I ask.
"Three," he says, sucking noisily on a tooth.
"Don't remember, but I've heard about it
from my folks. They're getting old."
He turns toward me and winks, as if to say *forgetful*.
His parents must be about my age. I look outside.
Radio monks wail an ominous hymn in the lull
of the conversation. I know these streets,
I grew up around here. Thirty-seven years ago
I had to run away, save myself from a country
that would rather torture and jail me
than let me live the life I wanted.

The chestnut trees I left behind as saplings
have now grown stout-domed crowns
full of spire-like white blossoms.
I can still feel the past dread I felt
on days when, passing this very place
I was stopped by the surly armed guards,
interrogated, frisked, as if I were the enemy,
while on my way back from school, or friends,
or work, terrified my thoughts could be read
on my face.

The car speeds up, the driver rants
about how much worse, how much better.
I pay no attention. We take a right turn
toward the park, then a left
in front of the newly renovated century-old
church I used to go to secretly at night
on Easter Eves, another right turn
on my street.

He stops, I pay, and as I exit, I point
to the crucifixes, the icons crowding his dashboard,
and say, "He sure is turning over in his grave
to know a thirty-three-year-old man owns
his own taxi and drives listening
to Christian sermons, brandishing
his freedom of religion. At your age,
on these streets, had I tried that,
I would have been arrested."

A total eclipse of the sun

On this side of town the streets
have not changed much. Indifferent,
they take my hurry without ever knowing
the hunger that brings me back—
the fear that a beloved place could be lost;
its scents, its colors, forgotten.

In the fifteen years I've been away,
the hundred-year-old buildings have remained
just as ancient. The sweet, camphorate incenses
of Balkan gardens slowly stir
a summer-brewed day. Under my soles I feel
the road's curved vertebrae—cobblestones,
and with each stone I step on, a story
takes me back to the linden-shaded house
of my childhood. All that I lived
within the walls of this house! Who can part
with the past without nostalgia?

This is the place I held as honestly dear
as my own name, yet it told something simpler,
something that did not change with intonations
and voices. This was home—the outer skin
that sheltered me from the fear of living
like an amulet cast against amnesia
and abandonment.

From the old attic comes an owl's bemoaning,
faint like the early dawn, and I am suddenly
surrounded by the past—Nana's frail hands
lacing my black-lacquered shoes; Mother

pouring milk in a tall glass; Father waltzing me
in his arms; the spiderwebs blooming
in the noon light; Brother shouting after me
in the park: *come home, come home*;
none of it by any chronology, as though
all these years my life piled up without order,
only to surface now, here,
while the sun is swiftly swallowed up
by a slab of dark in the middle of the day—
just as it had been predicted long ago—
a total eclipse, like the one I had seen
as a child, in this house.

But years do not go by
without taking their toll. Everything bears witness
to what has gone by: the granite steps to the door
are smoothly grooved; there are traces
of fingermarks on the walls; splashes of dried muck.
The rutted driveway dons a symmetry
of muddled wheels, saplings have grown old,
gardens aged.

Once the darkness lifts, I remember how
to tilt my head at just the right angle to see
a fine web shining in the noon's light
on the upper corner of the red-lacquered door—
the orb-weaving spider, warmed
by the newly recovered sun, knits
a wide doily of air with its wispy legs. Someplace
in its precise net, in the intricate scheme
created from instinct, death lies like a slice of night.

I know there is always an explanation,
other than prophecy or fate, but who could accept
without alarm the unruliness of our memories,
the coincidences, premonitions, afterthoughts,
the noon darkness of a summer day, as if,
within visions of the future, certain, foreseen,
the constant gloom of our destiny awaits us?

Who can honestly claim to be at ease
knowing how life, this given, becomes shorter
each time we tell a story from the past—
God Almighty, where did it all go?

The old house

I was barely twenty when I first stepped
on the stone path along hortensia shrubs
your mother fed a purple-ink concoction
she hoped would turn the efflorescence
from white to brilliant blue.

My stomach somersaulted once or twice,
but your parents welcomed me, and ever after
I had my own place at the oval table
next to sons, uncles, nieces; savoring
your mom's signature dishes.

We lived here for a while, then returned
on vacations, bringing our kids to spend time
with grandparents. Up there on the third floor
the small square window lit
the quaint bedroom-under-eaves,
smelling of dry pine and lavender,
with the pulsating colors of sunsets in mid-May.
We used to cuss the wistful dove-calls
rousing us at sunrise, after nights of parties
and lovemaking.

Munching on heart-shaped berries picked
from the thicket growing near the kitchen door,
we always had enough time to admire
the tapestries embroidered by a great-grandaunt;
or your father's famous rugby trophies.

After lunch we dozed under the picture windows
on the sofa's feathered pillows, and late nights
we listened to stories—your mother's lonely,
cloistered youth, your father's rowdy army days;
the many ancestors who passed, lifetimes before us.
On lazy autumn afternoons,
beneath the fragrant quince trees
in the orchard, we laughed, deciphering
the loud slurred calls of Gypsy peddlers.
This was the one spot on earth where I felt
I could bask in the quiet balance of the love
and acceptance I had been craving
since childhood.

The house lost its owners
to age and inheritance quarrels.
Deserted and alone, it defies winds,
freezing rains, heat waves.
The attic's caved-in roof, gaps
around windowsills allow the cold
to waft in, settle on the shut furnace,
the burst pipes, inside dusty cupboards.
I close my eyes, try to hear kids' bare feet
on granite stairs, but the laughter
of the children we were and the children we had
in this house fades, slips out the broken windows,
the blown roof tiles, while a gray November lies
crestfallen on the garden overrun by weeds,
wilted blue flowers, and brambles full of thorns,
where not one heart-shaped raspberry is left.

Dowry

Nona, I went back to our childhood street.
Your old house, what is left of it,
grows more decrepit under a wilderness
of vines and grasses gone to seed.
The guest room's shutters are still down,
but the walls crumble with each winter. No one
is left there, and no new owner claims the place.

Like me, you had to run away from a world
frozen in the Cold War, go someplace
where houses get rebuilt. Yet it's enough
to close my eyes and see the three
gray stone steps to your entrance,
the windows' heavy dark wood frames
drowsily peeking out from under the red clay tiles
of the slanted roof; the brass doorknobs,
the cool hallway with its pink mosaic floor
reflected in the intricate Venetian mirror,
the many rooms we played in.

Remember? The bustling kitchen
where your grandmother led an entire tribe
of self-assured women, your mother
and your aunts, fierce warriors armed
with spoons and rolling pins, jars, pots and pans,
in the battle to win the much-needed preserves
for the always coming, always endless, always hard
winter, while stuffing our always hungry mouths
with some just-made pie, and shooing us
out of there, into some other room to play.

Alas, how much we loved to eavesdrop
on their moralizing conversations and chew
the daily gossip! It's how we learned
that beauty in a woman should never show
much muscle, for sure the gymnast girls
would never marry, looking so masculine,
with their dark-tanned skin; that marriage
does not resolve desire, or else how to explain
mistresses, divorces; that husbands only think
they reign, while wives do the real ruling; that girls
should go as far as their brains can take them,
but remain chaste, pious, and primed
for motherhood. We mocked them, laughed,
incredulous, and ran to the quiet of the guest room,
where heavy shutters forever covered
the windows, as if a storm was imminent.

"Here," you showed me. "The dowry chests:
my grandmother's, my mother's, and mine."
Your grandma's, a large mahogany one
encrusted with pale mother-of-pearl,
was almost empty, only an elegant black dress
and leather shoes waited inside. "Her future
burial clothes," you said in passing.
Your mother's, made of lacquered cherrywood,
was still full with linens, silver, and porcelain cups.

Inside your white chest, among knickknacks
and lace curtains, you had hidden a world map,
a conversational guide, and a doll.

"She's going to be my only child," you whispered,
caressing its long woolen hair. "I want to travel."

We both knew travel was a forbidden dream
for those of us living behind the Iron Curtain,
but childhood knows no boundaries. Giggling,
I snatched the guide, and for hours we kept busy
learning how to ask for a cup of coffee in Italian,
Spanish, and Chinese. How old were we? Nine?
Ten? Not knowing whether we should love or fear
a future that seemed ordained, preserved
inside dowry chests full of linens
and outlawed dreams.

Inheritance

for Mădălina

We should be taking a picture,
you and I, the way it had been planned
for us when we were kids, to celebrate
growing up. Each Easter feast,
we had to put on a performance
for our family, gathered around their old,
to showcase their young.

Each one of us cousins had to present
our own small miracle—singing,
or counting, or pirouetting, to prove
whose smarts, or talents,
or beauty was inherited.

The two of us of the same age,
always competing—I'd sing like Grandpa,
you'd weave like Grandma. Grown,
I'd cook with Grandma's zest,
you'd garden with Grandfather's devotion.

In the very first pictures we lay
next to each other swaddled up like pupas
in white cocoons; our mothers
could not tell us apart. Milk sisters,
we were nursed together, sometimes swapped
between feedings from mother to mother.

Later, a fading black-and-white photo
shows us holding hands in the garden,
a blooming of gray shadows, a bit taller
year after year, until there are
no more pictures—the ritual—discontinued.
I left. The distance was too great
to be witnessed.

We should be taking a picture,
you and I, holding hands once again,
our children around us, performing
the miracle of resemblance:
my son has your wavy hair;
your daughter,
my dark, dreamy eyes.

We should try to find
Grandfather's garden
and pose in front of it
even if it has been divided,
like any inheritance.

Changed

for Coca

You tell me I haven't changed.
After all these many years I had to wear
new faces and learn strange tongues,
you say I haven't changed. And I know
you don't see the twenty-five-year-old
I was when I left; you see me as I am,
a grown woman, as you expected I
would become—a mother with no mother
near me, older—with no one from my tribe
close by, leading the way into old age.

What you don't see is how easy it is
to be back. I know what to say.
I know how to read inflections
and gestures; I regain the confidence
of my old habits, smile at people
I barely recognize, eat pizza
with fork and knife, and dessert
with a teaspoon, and no one
thinks me peculiar. Here,
when Mother sends me to fetch
herbs she wants for the meatballs,
I know exactly what spices she needs.

There is no dissonance in my speech,
and I seem to have caught on
to the new slang, so you say
I haven't changed.

I can't tell whom this deception
serves better, but it is soothing to both;
yet I know, on returning to that faraway
place you imagine as mine,
even if I said all the right words
there, my accent would always
give me away.

Exile, my country

Here I am,
my thin shadow staining the ground
of my return. No part of my fate clearer now
than at the time of departure. This shore,
a true Penelope, knows I am just another
warrior returned from one more burnt Troy,
yet, like any bird weary with flight, I take
the sight of my land as a sign of acceptance.

The tribe comes to greet me
in the pecking order of their love, eager to see
what I bring: small gifts, droll trifles,
untranslatable words, unfinished sentences,
a faulty memory, old prophecies.

The saffron-coated morning flickers
into clear sunlight. Lombardy poplars
lay melodious shadows over the house
of my childhood, and bit by bit, I recover
the tongue of my abandoned habits; remember
the peculiar wisdom, the indigenous creed
of my people.

Like a tribal chieftain, Father comes
cloaked in words filled with history,
to remind me that here is my fatherland.
Up in the attic a library stores several lives,
growth, loss.

"Here ..." he says,
with his ideal sense of tragedy,
"is the richer dust of your story. Your steps
resonate through the bones of your ancestors,
your stride cuts a path to their buried dreams.
Here, your blood ties you to the clay
you were made of. There are still wars
to be fought. You could pick up your life
from where you left it, a still-fitting uniform.
You could re-inhabit your absence. Take
the plow you abandoned in mid-furrow,
gather soil with your hands, and build
a living clump of clay for your roots,
or have you forgotten your roots?" he taunts,
illuminating the centuries of lives, deaths,
and wars melting on the dreary disorder
of our land. "Here ..." Father says.

But return admits no metaphor for itself.
All I've lived through, all that I've known—
the parting, the new land, the sea,
the journey back to my landlocked longing
for a home, all taught me
that even rebirth has limits.

What Father says sounds as simple
as a family name, but I know
the road he tries to make me walk on, first
in my mind, then with my soul, wishing
its archetypal structure could corrupt me again,

this road goes back, goes back to where I
don't belong anymore.

Here—I am a tree
whose seed never reached the ground.

Father says our tribe has been menaced
by poverty and wrongs, but exile
has stripped me so bare that the past peels
like a scab, while the clay I was made of
holds water or blood with the same indifference.

Here, the wavy country road taking me
to the place I once called mine
turns into an undulating graveyard
awaiting my prayers, while, like a bird
addicted to its migration,
I long for something simple
—an ocean, perhaps, or an equal oblivion.

The extinct homeland, a conversation with Czesław Miłosz

> "Tell me, as you would in the middle of the night
> When we face only night, the ticking of a watch,
> The whistle of an express train, tell me
> Whether you really think that this world
> Is your home?"
> — Czesław Miłosz, "An Appeal"

Home? Somewhere we belong? The metaphor
that includes us in its landscape? The place
that always takes us in, gives us context?
A land where no matter how scorched the soil,
our roots can still grow? Where all that we should,
could, would have been was realized? There is no
home for us, Czesław. There is no homeland.
Not anymore, not anywhere.
I wish I could learn to live with the malady
of an elsewhere, with the 'hidden certainty'
that trees grow taller, and the sunset's peacock tail
opens more intense colors over other horizons,
or else quit trying to understand *here* in contrast
to *there,* as if I never am where I am, as if I never
embody my own presence. I wish I could cease
craving the pathway to the physical place
I come from, and like nomads who don't know
where their exile started, I could accept amnesia
as enough of a birthplace.
Czesław, you've been at this game far longer than I;
tell me, is the elsewhere of our past homes real?
Or have I created a lucid paradise of what exists
only in memory? An obsessive echo,

like the brittle negative slide
of an otherwise ordinary picture.
Do I, haunted by the need for symmetry
in my narrative, hold real what I choose
to keep alive and harmonious through my story?
Do I, asking for the benefit of nostalgia—
a hallucination whose life is hunger
and thirst—break bread with Fata Morgana?

Fatherland—its cannibal mouth,
open like a graveyard, threatened to swallow me.
I ran away from my civilization, foolishly believing
I would be able to escape it, and emerge
from the narrow cocoon of my flight a butterfly
with no recollection of the caterpillar.
But no land lets itself be eradicated
without leaving behind fossils or ruins.
No new ground can compare
to what becomes sweeter when remembered.
Inscrutable, freed from its bitterness, my birthplace
turns into a garden, while the present,
always a temporary ark, is no salvation,
only a journey without a known destination.

I must have been kneaded out of a kind of clay
that doesn't stick to the potter's hands, is not one
with the rest of the earth, and just as wise words
don't keep the breath of the wise, my life,
once undone from its formative landscape
cannot be moored to a place anymore. Nor remain
part of the sword-laden history whose blood throbs

in my temples, nor to the ancestral oath
still awakening forgotten passions when I bite
into the bitter bread of a past ethnic pride,
not even to the vision of an alley
between columnar poplars.

All that I have are images, voices, and faces—
people and angels. A land that neither lives
nor dies, but endures crystallized, as static
as a picture. All there is, is a harsh saddle
I have not yet broken into, and the promise
of a mythology that does not sanctify people
trudging out of their burning pasts, a mythology
that does not describe fog-encircled forests
and rolling hills, but a calling, a thirst. Exiled,

I make a vow to be what I don't know to a land
I have not inherited, while the old homeland,
the one that becomes extinct in the distance,
survives only in my mouth, in the flavors
I long for, in the mother tongue I teach to my children.

There is no motherland. I am
its pre-existing condition. I am
the great-grandmother of someone who will never know
the exact place I came from, or why I had to run away,
or how I worshipped.

I am my own myth, the very first symbol,
as nebulous as any beginning.

The problem with Ithaka

"Keep Ithaka always in your mind.
Arriving there is what you're destined for.
But don't hurry the journey at all"
—C.P. Cavafy, "Ithaka"

All that has ever been told—
the war, the landlocked sea chanting with storms,
the right and the wrong reasons to pause
on narrow shores, to postpone the destination
for erroneous turns, the many gods asked to listen
to the eternal yearnings, all—is true.
And faithful in the distance, Ithaka—
sealed vision, awaits.

Ithaka—my luminous island
in the middle of a sea claimed as mine
through blood and birth. There,
bare-breasted alabaster goddesses clasp
serpents exquisitely coiled in front of gardens
and portals. Emerald salamanders dart out
of the cool shade. Sensuous paintings
enlighten alcoves, and seagulls
fly wide-winged shadows over rain-peppered sand.
There, young girls splash whitewash on the walls
to clean the winter's soot, fishermen
spill nets into the sea, and peasants
cut thick monastic bread, while the opulent dawn
spreads its blossom on the salt-soaked horizon.
Everything and everyone is there.

From the dark yeast of my return, I long
to be back and settle there,
between my old boundaries of right and wrong.

The road is long, strewn with unknown ports
lively with commerce, and merchants
offering mother-of pearl, ebony, seductive
perfumes; and I do take my time, cross
an insomniac sea, greedily tasting the life
sprouting avariciously around. I get rich
with wisdom on the way to the place I keep
in my mind as my destined ground, while the sky
strides forward with wet birds flying tall arches,
restless and weary. Amid fluorescent foam
and the sea's vociferous slang, Ithaka remains
the only language broad enough to shelter
all my longings. And finally, I disembark.

Stranded like the sand between sea and land, impatient,
I search for the usual illusion—friends, houses, people,
and gardens, thinking the void is behind me.
But all I find is my own ghost—what I would
have become had I stayed in the world that exists
only in the mementos kept by those who lived
long enough to see me return.

O, Ithaka goes on being Ithaka, all right.
It takes me in as its Lazarus returned from the dead,
long after Life has healed his absence
into a scar of myth.

Simon Says

The game remains the same:
a pebble skimmed across the water
glides for you as it did for your father.
Playing charades near skyscrapers,
your fingers, gauzy for a moment in the sun,
change words to gestures I mimed
in my grandfather's orchard.

Airplanes have changed shapes
since my imaginary flights,
but outstretched arms
and a slow diving motion of your head
still does the trick, and it flies you
to another world.

Alas, nothing remains
of the carriage wheels' rumble,
the clip-clop of horse-trot
on flagstone roads, nothing
remains of the Gypsy peddler's calls
selling topsoil with his voice;
the lament of his slurred vowels
making *soil* sound like *soul*;
nothing remains of the harness bells,
or the dust-ghosts soaring
behind horseshoes.

But it was life,
not even long ago.

I trusted the day would rise
from night, just 'cause it always did;
a thatched roof kept winter out;
the wood barrel collected raindrops
to keep them holy; goose feathers
were forever white; a moon-faced rock
tied to the well's thick chain balanced
the heavy bucket above the deep
waterlogged underworld.

I saved chunks of charred wood
to scribble secret messages to friends;
you type slang on the computer
a conversation with your schoolmates
about a picture in a textbook,
a faraway country of thatched roofs
and gravel roads traveled by Gypsies
selling topsoil; your teacher called it
"the Old World." Remember,
that, for me, is childhood.

Bilingualism, a legacy

Think of it as changing codes, the lecturer says.

The image of the eager little girl I was
comes back to me. On Mother's lap she speaks
words in German, in Hungarian. Mother tongues,
tongues I no longer understand.

The window of opportunity closes at six, or seven.

I never learned to speak Hungarian, Yiddish,
German. The streets, the schools, the markets,
once a glorious and vibrant mix of sounds,
and lilts and twisting tongues
that enriched generations of ancestors
who lived for centuries in the same house,
grew quiet before I was born in Great-
grandmother's peacock-blue bedroom.

*Neuroscientists believe the brains of bilinguals
show more plasticity, are resilient.*

The songs, the stories, the fables spiced
with their own native accents and inflections,
told by sages and minstrels straddling two,
three languages at once, were stifled
into a *national language*.

*It is about being able to hear and use more sounds
and inflections.*

When I turned four, my multilingual mother,
caught in the ethnic struggles between Romanians,
Germans, Hungarians, decided I should not
have to fear the perils of a *minority* identity.
She stopped teaching me her mother tongues.
Her way of trying to survive the legacy of war,
her missing, murdered family, the chauvinist regime.
I had no grandparents to teach me,
not much of a community of speakers left alive
after the war. I grew up monolingual
in Romanian—beautiful, rich, lonely language.

It doesn't matter if the child acquires fluency.

Later in life, exiled from my native land, I had
to learn English while teaching Romanian
to my kids. I speak Romanian
to my toddler grandson now. I quiz him playfully:
"How do you say *red?*" "I don't like to say *rosu,*"
he says. "I don't like to say v*erde,*" and goes on
listing in Romanian all the colors he doesn't *like*
to say.

I laugh, hug him, whisper *bobocul meu frumos,
pui dulce,*[5] tender words in the old tongue,
and wonder, should he one day look back in time,
will he hear my voice, the language? Will he
remember? Will he understand?

[5]My beautiful bud, my sweet pup.

After visiting the National Immigration Museum

on Ellis Island, where my friend Cher and I
playfully imagined long-lost ancestors
smiling back at us from the nineteenth century
(a townswoman, on a fading ferrotype, donning
a feathered hat, looked like Cher; a Gypsy matron,
smoking a long pipe, looked like me)
we find ourselves in bumper-to-bumper traffic
on the turnpike.

It is the end of a hot August day. I pay attention
to the road and disregard the exhaust, the nasty
NY drivers fishtailing brazenly to gain a few inches
of space. Inside the air-conditioned car,
Cher tells me she believes in reincarnation,
mentions Babylonian gods, Egyptian myths,
transmigration, trying to elicit more
than just a raised eyebrow on my part.

At the edge of the highway, the meadow
sparkles russet in the sunset.
Five great blue herons rise above low-tide waters
and quivering reeds. Their wide wingspan,
their ease of movement, make me wish
I too could escape the smog and the rush hour.

I listen to Cher politely,
unconvinced—parallel universes, past lives.
Suddenly, she asks: "If it were possible,
what would you like to come back as?"

Really? Is this how
the physical reality's discomfort
and disappointments get solved?
The perfect afterlife reclaimed
as a different shape, in a different era,
as a second chance?

"I'd like to come back as a song," I say.
"Who needs to live again the doom
of a decaying body?" But then I see myself
at eleven, in the ballet studio,
dark hair pulled back in a low bun, glowing
peach complexion, dressed in a sleek white leotard,
a vaporous silk skirt and satin slippers,
dancing alone reflected in a wall-sized mirror—
the balancé, the brisé, the arabesque.

Long limbs, narrow waist, budding breasts,
the grace of an ephemeral body
at its most vulnerable, fleeting age,
no longer a child, not yet a woman, deep
in concentration, in search
of unreachable perfection.
Yet, only now, looking back,
I savor the beauty of it all.

Ex-pats

Look at us here, at a backyard barbecue
in Nutley, NJ, filling the air with our *native*
aphorisms while guffawing at the awkwardness
of newly acquired idioms like *rubberneck,*
and cooking *from scratch.* We scoff

at the uncouthness of holding one's hand
in one's lap when eating at the table (what
is that hand doing down there?). We snigger
at the New World's words and customs
that still remain stubbornly foreign to us.

We're all past the halfway mark
of any expectations. Some *arrived*, some
are still working on whatever they were
going to be as grownups (which me?).
We watch our children enter an adulthood

we barely comprehend, becoming what we
have not dreamed or dared becoming. Back
in the Old Country no one knows us anymore,
no one speaks our language, no one shares
our longings. Listen to us reminisce

about the *traditional* summer-camp snack—
the one sticky cube of fruit-flavored
Turkish Delight between two tasteless,
often moldy, hardtacks. We must be the last
bearers of that memory.

Back there, those we left behind
changed the world so much so
that, on returning, we get lost in the new
language grown in our absence, lost
walking the childhood streets demolished,
rebuilt, renamed, into a landscape
we can't recognize.

We keep the past in our minds
with its names, its quaint customs,
just as we keep the faces
of those departed alive in our souls,
while Motherland survives only here,
in Nutley, among her aging ex-pats
indulging in nostalgia.

The way we were

There was a time
when we talked about right
and wrong in theoretical terms
as approximate as any lack
of experience. About love
as if it were only an intense idea,
all details as inconsequential
as the early dew.

There was a time when we stood
resolute, ready to die for freedom,
however abstract; when we thought
courage was enough of a legacy,
and would have liked to be remembered
for being lighthearted, telling witty tales,
clever jokes, concocting funny curses.

There was a time when reinventing
whatever came to hand—language,
food, fashion, the meaning of love,
or of friendship, was as quintessential
as naming constellations. The words alone
were a dizzying wine.

There was a time when our parents
worried about the price of meat,
while they lined up, covered by the early-
morning dew, in front of empty bread stores
to make sure there was food on the table.

Now we throw our arms up in the air,
dismayed when confronted with a rose
tattooed on our teenage daughter's body,
and, worried, we lecture and rant on the perils
of hepatitis, while making our children promise
they'll consider details, consequences.

Now we wake up ready to weigh
the price of a daily meal, and smile,
seeing the pearly dew, as if *it*
were the only true shining.

All we have

is a duffle bag of stories,
heirlooms,
and memorized geography.

Should anyone show us
how the landscape, the inhabitants
of our past have changed,

the faint illusion
of belonging,
of clinging on
to what gives us context,
would break like a mirror
into thousands of angular shreds
of skewed images.

I plead to be allowed nostalgia—
the small, pleasantly sad
souvenir tucked away
in a personal history
that has to be accepted
and is immutable.

Poem for a great-grandchild

Let her have time, and silence,
enough paper to make mistakes and go on.
—Jane Hirshfield, "The Poet"

One day I will be your past. One part
of that perfect spiral—your own genes'
microscopic memory. One day
I will be your homework—that silly project
my son, your grandfather, had once:
write about your great-grandmother.

How will you imagine me? Will you
say I was a foreigner? Stranger
to this land of pilgrims' pride? Will you
tell of my broken tongue? The many
mistakes in my speech would have reached you
hemmed in family anecdotes.

Will you tell I went on? Combing
dictionaries and thesauruses
like one combs a beach for the perfect
oyster shell; only, I tried to find
a new language and make it my own
in this place, this life story captured

in family photographs like this one,
where I bend over a notebook as the clock
near the study-room window marks every
passing second of the night with a stab-like
noise. The silk-shaded ivory lamp dissolves

its honey-glow light into the smooth warmth
of the oak table, the wooden chair squeaks
every time I shift my body in search of comfort,

or the best word, and the quick-moving
shadow of my hand stains the paper
before my thoughts do. The ones I love,
asleep in the dark room behind me,
think in a language I do not own,
while on my tongue poems decipher
the words of my dreams.

One day, you, child,
in a world I can only imagine,
will read my poems, will think my words,
will find me.

Acknowledgments

Grateful thanks to the editors of the following journals where some of these poems first appeared, sometimes in different versions and/or with different titles:

War, Literature, & the Arts, Pinyon, Visions International, North American Review, Argestes, Paterson Literary Review, Timber Creek Review, The Salt River Review, Into the Teeth of the Wind, Asphodel, Tapestry, The Hidden Oak, Blueline, American Diaspora: Poetry of Exile, The Red White and Blue, Approaching Literature in the Twenty-first Century, Caustic Frolic, Red Wheelbarrow, Woman Ages Anthology, Muddy River Poetry Review, US1 Worksheets, Verse-Virtual, Rockvale Review, Spire Light Journal, Nonbinary Review, Syncopation Literary Journal, Ancient Paths Online, and *Consequence Forum.*

The poems "Top-Secret Report," "Expelled—Bucharest, 1970s," "Tante Lori," "Roof over far away," and "Bilingualism, a legacy" also appear in the chapbook *The Later Generation*, published by Kelsay Books in 2024.

Shout-outs

Mii de multumiri (that's "a thousand thanks" in Romanian) to the many poets and writers I have encountered along my journey: Roberta Greening and the members of the Bergen Poets Workshop, Barry Sheinkopf and The Writing Center, The Red Wheelbarrow Poets, Cafe Blue Writers, the past and present members of the crewrt-l email group, Alicia Ostriker, Ann Fisher-Wirth, Wendy Taylor Carlisle, Penelope Schott, Athena Kildegaard, Barbara Taylor, Barbara Leiding, Jimmy Roberts, Maria Lisella, Ann Settel, Jeff Steinberg, Arlene Metrick, Annette Hollander, Deborah Zeigler, and Mary Himmelweit. Without their help, patience, intellectual honesty, warmth, and encouragement, I never could have been able to go on.

And to you, dear friends: Doinița, Mihnea, Tamara, Gary, Cicu, Ileana, Ducu, Mihaela, Coca, Virginia, Andrei, Roby, Bogdan, Hedda, Petrică, Peggy, Mark, Sondra, Lisa, Richard, Cathy … and many more, too many to mention, a big thank you for being near me when I needed you, and for having been witnesses, companions, and part of this 'legend.' This book is for you too.

Also, heartfelt thanks to my copy editor, Cindy Hochman, of "100 Proof" Copyediting Services, who went above and beyond her professional duties to help bring this book into being, and becoming a dear and trusted friend in the process.

About the Author

Ana Doina is a Romanian-born American writer living in New Jersey. She holds a Master of Arts in History and Philosophy from Bucharest University. Due to political and social pressures, she had to leave Romania during the Ceaușescu regime.

Growing up after the Holocaust and during the Cold War, as the inheritor of that tormented past, Ana Doina is exploring through poetry the lament and the wisdom left behind by that history. As an emigrant/immigrant poet she writes about her personal experiences of losing and finding the elusive *at-home* state of awareness humans need in order to live and thrive.

Her poems have appeared in numerous national and international print and online magazines, anthologies, and textbooks. In the last thirty years she has been, at one time or another, one of the coordinators of the group Bergen Poets, a New Jersey community-based poetry organization; the leader of Leonia Poetry Forum, a community-based poetry study group; and a workshop instructor in the JOY poetry workshop for the Oakland, NJ, Middle School District. One of her poems won Honorable Mention in the Anna Davidson Rosenberg Awards for Poems on the Jewish Experience contest in 2007 and three of her poems were nominated for the 2000, 2002, and 2004 Pushcart Prizes. Her chapbook, *The Later Generation*, was published by Kelsay Books in 2024.